Dublin Great Britain. Treasury. Committee to inquire into the Regis

Registry of Deeds Office, Dublin

Dublin Great Britain. Treasury. Committee to inquire into the Regis

Registry of Deeds Office, Dublin

ISBN/EAN: 9783741198663

Manufactured in Europe, USA, Canada, Australia, Japa

Cover: Foto ©Andreas Hilbeck / pixelio.de

Manufactured and distributed by brebook publishing software
(www.brebook.com)

Dublin Great Britain. Treasury. Committee to inquire into the Regis

Registry of Deeds Office, Dublin

REPORT

FROM THE

SELECT COMMITTEE

ON

PUBLICATION OF PRINTED PAPERS;

WITH THE

MINUTES OF EVIDENCE,

AND APPENDIX.

Ordered, by The House of Commons, *to be Printed*,
8 *May* 1837.

Jovis, 16° die Februarii, 1837.

Ordered, THAT a Select Committee be appointed to examine Precedents with respect to the Circulation and Publication of Reports and Papers printed by Order of this House, and to ascertain the *Law and Practice* of Parliament prior to and since the Order for the Sale of such Papers.

And a Committee was appointed, of—

Lord Viscount Howick.
Sir Robert Peel.
Mr. Attorney-General.
Mr. C. W. Williams Wynn.
Mr. Tancred.
Sir William Follett.
Mr. Charles Villiers.
Sir Frederick Pollock.
Mr. Roebuck.
Lord Stanley.
Sir George Strickland.
Sir Robert Harry Inglis.
Mr. Serjeant Wilde.
Sir George Clerk.
Mr. O'Connell.

Ordered, THAT the said Committee have power to send for Persons, Papers and Records.

Ordered, THAT Five be the Quorum of the Committee.

Veneris, 3° die Martii, 1837.

Ordered, THAT the Committee have power to report their Proceedings and Opinion from time to time to the House.

Ordered, THAT the Petition of Messrs. Hansard (presented 6th February last) be referred to the Committee.

PROCEEDINGS OF THE COMMITTEE.

Martis, 21° die Februarii, 1837.

Present:

Lord Viscount Howick in the Chair.

Mr. Attorney-General.
Sir Frederick Pollock.
Sir George Strickland.
Sir Robert H. Inglis.
Lord Stanley.
Mr. Tancred.

Jovis, 9° die Martii, 1837.

Lord Viscount Howick in the Chair.

Mr. Attorney-General.
Sir Robert H. Inglis.
Sir Frederick Pollock.
Mr. C. W. Williams Wynn.
Sir George Clerk.
Sir Robert Peel.
Lord Stanley.
Mr. Serjeant Wilde.

Mercurii, 15° die Martii, 1837.

Lord Viscount Howick in the Chair.

Mr. Attorney-General.
Sir Robert Peel.
Mr. Tancred.
Mr. Serjeant Wilde.
Sir William Follett.
Sir George Strickland.
Mr. C. W. Williams Wynn.

Lunæ, 20° die Martii, 1837.

Lord Viscount Howick in the Chair.

Sir Robert H. Inglis.
Mr. C. W. Williams Wynn.
Mr. Tancred.
Mr. Serjeant Wilde.

Sabbati, 22° die Aprilis, 1837.

Lord Viscount Howick in the Chair.

Sir George Strickland.
Sir Frederick Pollock.
Mr. C. W. Williams Wynn.
Sir William Follett.
Lord Stanley.
Sir George Clerk.
Mr. Serjeant Wilde.
Mr. Attorney-General.
Sir R. H. Inglis.
Mr. O'Connell.
Sir R. Peel.
Mr. Charles Villiers.

Resolutions moved by Sir Robert H. Inglis:

That the Privileges claimed by this House from The King at the opening of each Parliament, and granted by The King, and also the other Privileges pertaining to this House, which have been recognized by the Courts of Law within this realm (the same being Privileges for maintaining the freedom of debate within this House, and the security of the persons of Members thereof from arbitrary violence, and from all arrest except by courts of law for contempt or in execution of criminal process), are essentially necessary to the existence and integrity of this House, as a body summoned to counsel The King touching the arduous affairs of Church and State; and that any person offending against such Privileges is guilty of a violation of the Law of Parliament.

That the right to punish persons guilty of such offence, whether such offence were by interrupting the freedom of debate within the House, either by direct violence or by threats to any Member thereof, or by publishing any libel against the proceedings of this House, or were by contempt of the House before it, or were by arrest of any Member thereof, other than in execution of lawful process as aforesaid, hath been repeatedly claimed and enforced by the authority of this House, and that no other authority hath or ought to have any jurisdiction whatever in limiting the exercise of the powers of this House, in punishing all persons so offending.

That

That although this House hath occasionally addressed The King, to direct His Majesty's Attorney-General to prosecute offenders for publishing libels against the proceedings of this House, yet that this House hath likewise an undoubted right to inquire into all libels against its authority or proceedings, and to punish the same accordingly as breaches of its Privileges.

That no Member of this House hath any claim of Privilege in respect to the publication of any matter or thing purporting to be his Speech, which, by due course of law, may be found to be a libel; and that this House hath never interfered, and ought not to interfere, in any legal proceedings instituted thereon.

That this House doth not claim any right, and that no other body of His Majesty's subjects hath any right, to publish any matter or thing, which by law would be adjudged to be a libel if contained in an unauthorized publication, or to do anything which by law would be adjudged to be trespass or any personal injury.

That the Printing of Papers presented to this House, whether the same be Accounts, Reports or otherwise, is, and ought to be, for the use of Members of this House, and as such, ought to be Publication Privileged; but that any sale or dispersal of such Papers to any but to Members of this House, is, and ought to be, Publication Not Privileged.

That while this House will resent and resist every attempt on the part of others to libel its proceedings, it doth not claim, and ought not to claim, any exemption on the part of its Speaker, or of any of its Officers, from any legal liability to which its proceedings may be subject; and that any Publication which would be a libel against an individual if proceeding from another individual, is a libel if published by this House, any claim of Privilege notwithstanding, except as aforesaid; and that any act which would be adjudged by law to be a trespass or personal injury if committed by an individual, is a trespass or personal injury if committed by Order of this House, any claim of Privilege notwithstanding, except as aforesaid.

Question put, that the Committee do agree to these Resolutions:

Aye.	Noes.
Sir R. H. Inglis.	Sir George Strickland.
	Sir Frederick Pollock.
	Mr. C. W. Williams Wynn.
	Sir William Follett.
	Lord Stanley.
	Sir George Clerk.
	Mr. Serjeant Wilde.
	Mr. Attorney-General.
	Mr. O'Connell.
	Sir Robert Peel.

Motion made and Question proposed by Sir Frederick Pollock, to leave out Paragraph 42.

Question put, that Paragraph 48 stand part of the Report:

Ayes.	Noes.
Mr. Charles Villiers.	Lord Stanley.
Mr. Attorney-General.	Mr. O'Connell.
Mr. Serjeant Wilde.	Sir G. Strickland.
Mr. C. W. Williams Wynn.	Sir William Follett.
	Sir George Clerk.
	Sir Robert Peel.
	Sir Frederick Pollock.

Martis, 9° die Maii, 1837.

Lord Viscount Howick in the Chair.

Mr. C. W. Williams Wynn.	Lord Stanley.
Sir Robert Peel.	Mr. Charles Villiers.
Mr. Serjeant Wilde.	Sir Frederick Pollock.
Sir William Follett.	

R E P O R T.

THE SELECT COMMITTEE appointed "to examine Precedents with respect to the CIRCULATION and PUBLICATION of REPORTS and PAPERS, Printed by Order of this House, and to ascertain the Law and Practice of Parliament prior to and since the Order for the Sale of such Papers," and who were empowered to report their Proceedings and Opinions from time to time to the House; and to whom the Petition of James Hansard and Luke G. Hansard (presented 6th February) was referred:——HAVE examined the matters to them referred, and have agreed to the following REPORT:

1. YOUR Committee having been appointed for the purposes above mentioned, in consequence of the recent proceedings at Nisi Prius, in the case of *Stockdale* v. *Hansard* and others, and of the direction of the Lord Chief Justice of the King's Bench to the jury, "That the fact of the House of Commons having directed Messrs. Hansard to publish all their Parliamentary Reports is no justification for them, or for any bookseller who publishes a Parliamentary Report containing a Libel against any man," are strongly impressed with the conviction that the duty imposed upon them is vitally connected with the independence of Parliament, and with the maintenance of that power by which alone it can retain the means of wise and satisfactory Legislation, and they have endeavoured to present to the House, in the most perspicuous form, the information they have collected upon the matter submitted to them; and with that view have directed their attention to the following subjects: Appendix, No. 1, p. 63.

2. *First.*—The date of the earliest orders for *Printing* given by this House, and its practice on this subject.

3. *Secondly.*—The degree of publicity which has at different periods been given to Papers printed by order of this and the other House of Parliament.

4. *Thirdly.*—The Manner in which the recent Order of this House, for the Printing and Circulation of its Reports and Papers, has been carried into effect.

5. *Fourthly.*—Whether Papers printed for the House have been held to afford grounds for legal proceedings prior to the case of *Stockdale* v. *Hansard*, and what would be the effect of the principles laid down in that case: and—

6. *Lastly.*—Your Committee have stated to the House what appears to them to be the Law and Practice of Parliament, in regard to the matter of Privilege, to the elucidation of which their inquiries have been directed.

---

7. The imperfect manner in which the Journals of the Houses of Parliament were formerly kept, many important transactions being wholly omitted, and others so briefly entered as not to furnish the means of appreciating their effects,

effect, and the destruction of the Records and Documents by the late fire of the Two Houses of Parliament, have compelled Your Committee to resort for information to widely-dispersed materials, to which there are no convenient means of reference.

Sources of information.

8. The sources from which Your Committee have obtained the greater part of the facts detailed in their Report, are, 1st, the Journals of the Two Houses of Parliament; 2dly, the Collection of Tracts and Parliamentary Papers in the Library of this House, including a volume of Votes and Proceedings of the years 1680 and 1681, presented by the Right Honourable C. W. Williams Wynn, M.P.; and, 3dly, the Collection of Tracts in the British Museum, which consists in part of Original Papers printed by the Houses of Parliament, but these being bound up with miscellaneous matter, it is difficult to collect from them materials applicable to any particular subject.

PRINTING.

Commencement of Journals.

9. The Journals of this House commence in 1547, and continue down to the present time; but the course of entering the Proceedings has varied from time to time, both in regularity and form; the entries being much more specific and detailed at some periods than at others. The earliest entry contained in them, relating to the *Printing* of any Parliamentary Papers, is on the 30th July 1641; when the House adopted certain Resolutions, and ordered that they should be printed.

2 Com. Journ. p. 230.

10. From 1641 to 1680, there are various resolutions for the printing of specific Votes and Papers.

Appx. (A.) No. 1, p. 19, and Appx. No. 3, p. 71.

11. In 1680–1, a *general* resolution was adopted for printing the Votes and Proceedings of the House; and from that year such general Order has been renewed every Session, and a Printer appointed for the purpose by The Speaker, an occasional prohibition being added against all other persons printing the same; Reports and Miscellaneous Parliamentary Papers have also been from time to time printed under distinct Orders of the House. The practice thus detailed has been continued up to the present time.

Appx. (A.) No. 2, p. 21, par. 98.

12. The only exception to the continuance of this practice was in the year 1702, when the general order for printing the Votes and Proceedings was for a very short period suspended; but even during this interruption of the printing of the Votes, there were several instances of special orders for printing other Papers. The circumstances accompanying this temporary discontinuance are stated in the Appendix.

PUBLICATION.

13. The next and most important point of inquiry is, whether the Papers printed by order of the House were so for the exclusive use of its Members or for general Publication?

4 Com. Journ. p. 290, &c.

14. No doubt can exist that it was with a view to the latter object, that the practice of Printing was introduced. This is shown by the subsequent Proceedings of the House with regard to the Order for Printing of 1641 above referred to, and by the appointment of a Committee in the subsequent year to consider, among other things, "the best way of divulging, dispersing and publishing the Orders and Votes, and also the Declarations of the House, through the kingdom, and of the well and true Printing of them."

Ib. p. 609. 618.

15. This Committee presented on the 6th June an Order for dispersing and divulging the Orders and Declarations of the House through the Sheriffs, Under-sheriffs, Constables, Headboroughs and Tithingmen of the several Counties,

Counties, with directions for the speedy *Publication* to the Inhabitants; and on the 9th of June the Committee made Reports, whereupon it was resolved that certain Examinations, Remonstrances, Orders, Votes and Declarations should be printed and *published*, and an Order was made for the payment of the expense.

16. Your Committee think it right to remark, that the mode of publication through the sheriffs and other local officers may probably have been adopted from usage of an earlier date. Although no entry on the Journals or other record has been found respecting the Publication of the Proceedings of Parliament prior to 1640, yet it scarcely admits a doubt, that from a much earlier period Parliament must occasionally have found it necessary or expedient that particular proceedings should be made public, although the means by which it was done cannot be traced; but as Acts of Parliament were anciently published at the county courts and other local tribunals, it is not improbable that the same channel of communication was used; and that hence might be derived the course adopted in regard to the first Order for Printing in 1641, which, it will be observed, was accompanied by directions that the papers ordered to be printed should be sent to the sheriffs, under-sheriffs, constables, headboroughs and tithingmen, and who were required to publish the same to the inhabitants in the respective districts. It is easy to imagine that the increased facilities afforded by printing would be substituted for the ancient and less convenient mode.

1 Blackstone's Com. p. 185.

Appx. (A.) No. 1, p. 19.

9 Com. Jour. p. 604. 609. 616.

17. After the Restoration, the practice of publishing Papers printed for the House continued. The debate in 1680–1, upon the motion to print the Votes and Proceedings, was published contemporaneously; it is to be found in Mr. C. Williams Wynn's volume, and is copied into the Parliamentary History. The declared object of the Motion was the *Publication* of the Proceedings, and the professional members then in the House urged no objection upon any legal ground; the opposition was confined to Mr. Secretary Jenkins, himself an eminent lawyer and politician, who resisted it on the ground that it *was an appeal to the people*, unsuited to the gravity of the House. The whole debate is so applicable and full of interest, that Your Committee, unwilling to abbreviate it, have given it entire in the note below.*

Appx. (A.) No. 2. 9 Com. Jour. 649. and S. G. (Speaker's Gallery) Collection, vol. 76.

Par. Hist. 4 vol. p. 1306.

18. In

* Debate on Printing the Votes, March 24, 1680–1.

Sir John Hotham.—What I am about to move concerns us all. The last Parliament, when you were moved to print your Votes, it was for the security of the nation, and you found it so; it prevented ill representations of us to the world by false copies of our Votes, and some deprived your honour in the care of it; and I am confident that this House will be no more ashamed of their actions than the last was. Printing our Votes will be for the honour of the King and safety of the nation. I am confident, if it had been necessary, you would have had petitions from the parts I come from, that your actions might be made public. As I came hither, everybody almost that I met upon the road cried, God bless you. I move, therefore, "that your Votes may be ordered to be printed with the rest of your proceedings." And I shall only add, that yourself has done so well in taking that care upon you the last Parliament, that the House will desire you to continue them in the same method.

Sir William Cowper.—That which put me upon moving the printing your Votes the last Parliament, was false papers that went about in former Parliaments of the Votes and Transactions of the House. Let men think what they please, the weight of England is the people; and the world will find that they will sink Popery at last. Therefore I second the motion.

Mr. Sec. Jenkins.—I beg pardon, if I consent not to the motion. Consider the gravity of this assembly. There is no great assembly in Christendom that does it. It is against the gravity of this assembly, and it is a sort of appeal to the people. It is against your gravity, and I am against it.

Mr. Boscawen.—If you had been a Privy Council, then it were fit what you do should be kept secret; but your Journal Books are open, and copies of your Votes in every coffee-house, and if you print them not, *half* votes will be dispersed to your prejudice. This printing is like plain Englishmen, who are not ashamed of what they do, and the people you represent will have a true account of what you do. You may prevent publishing what parts of your transactions you will, and print the rest.

Mr. L. Gower.—I find that those who write our Votes and Transactions, and send them all England over, are favoured; and I believe that no gentleman in the House will be against printing them but Jenkins. I hope you will not be ashamed of what you do; therefore I am for printing your Votes.

Colonel

Appx. No. 3, p. 73.

18. In Mr. C. Williams Wynn's volume, No. 7, December 9th, 1680, is contained the Resolution of the House, ordering Dangerfield's Narrative (relative to the Meal-tub Plot) to be printed and published, and that Dangerfield should have the benefit of the Printing, which shows an extensive sale to have been anticipated.

Appx. (B.)

Appx. No. 3, p. 71 to 78.

19. From 1641 till past the middle of the last century, many of the Papers printed by order of the House purport, upon the face of them, to be printed and published "by Order,"* with the name of the Clerk of the House attached, and they usually had the appointment and prohibition of the Speaker with regard to Printing set out at the back of the title-page, sometimes with the note at the foot of the paper, "that the same was sold at, &c."—the establishment of the Printer appointed. These Papers being printed for and by the Order of the House, must have been constantly under its view, and the sale notorious, though no express order for it is to be found in the Journals.

Appx. No. 3, p. 73 to 78, and Appx. No. 4, p. 85, 88, 89, 90, 92.

20. The Sale of the Votes and Proceedings of the House by the Printer appears to have continued without interruption from its first commencement. At first the whole expense of Printing was thus defrayed, and a profit was derived from it, which was accounted for to the Speaker. Subsequently the expense of Printing having become more than the whole receipts from the sale, the account was transferred to the Treasury. Credit was given by the Printer for the sums received in payment for copies of the Votes sold by him, and the balance due to him, after deducting the amount, was paid by the public.

Appx. (A.) par. 50.

Appx. No. 3, p. 71, 79, 80 to 84.

Appx. No. 4, p. 85, Extracts from Reports 1801, (607.) 1807, (316.) 1818, (400.) 1831/2, (713.) 1833, (717.) (648.) 1835, (392.) (606.)

21. With respect to Reports and Miscellaneous Papers Printed for the House, the case was different; the sale to the public *by the Printer*, appears from the imprint on the Papers to have continued beyond the middle of the last century, and to have then ceased, though Your Committee have not been able to ascertain at what precise period. The number of copies of each paper which were printed continued always however to exceed the number of Members of the House, and varied according to the interest which, from the nature of the subject, the public might be supposed to take in the publication. The manner in which the distribution of these extra copies was effected in the interval between the cessation of the original practice of sale, and its resumption by the recent Order of August 1835, is detailed in the Reports of the several Committees which have had the subject of the Printed Papers under their deliberation.

22. Your

Colonel Mildmay.—By experience we have found, that when former Parliaments have been prorogued or dissolved, they have been sent away with a declaration against them. If our actions be naught, let the world judge of them; if they be good, let them have their virtue. It is fit that all Christendom should have notice of what you do, and posterity of *what you have done*, and I hope they will do as you do; therefore I am for printing the Votes.

Sir Francis Winnington.—Because what has been said by Jenkins is a single opinion; for he says "printing is an appeal to the people," I hope the House will take notice that printing our Votes is not contrary to law. But pray who sent us hither? The Privy Council is constituted by the King, but the House of Commons is by the choice of the people. I think it not natural nor rational, that the people who sent us hither should not be informed of our actions. In the Long Parliament it was a trade amongst clerks to write Votes, and it was then said by a learned gentleman, "that it was no offence to inform the people of Votes of Parliament, &c., and they ought to have notice of them." The Long Parliament were wise in their generation to conceal many things they did from the people; and the clerk who dispersed the Votes was sent away, and nothing done to him. The Popish party dread nothing more than printing what you do; and I dread that a man in Jenkins's post (and such an accusation upon him as is in the last Parliament) should hold such a position, "that printing your Votes was an appeal to the people."

Resolved, That the Votes and Proceedings of this House be printed.

Mr. Harbord.—Now you have passed this Vote, I would graft something upon it. I move "that the care of printing the Votes may be committed to The Speaker," who so well acquitted himself in in the last Parliament. Which was ordered.—*Parliamentary History*, vol. 4, p. 1306.

* The Committee have inserted in the Appendix an important Report upon a question of Privilege, the title-page of which they have caused to be reprinted in fac-simile.—Appendix (B.)

22. Your Committee find from these Reports, and from other Evidence, that the Miscellaneous Papers Printed for the House were, during the period now adverted to, made accessible to the public, partly by the sale of a certain number of copies, to which Officers of the House were entitled as perquisites, partly by gratuitous distribution under Orders from the Speaker, generally obtained by application to individual Members of the House.

Appendix, No. 4, p. 76, and App. No. 3, p. 84.

23. The obvious intention of the House that its Printed Papers should be in general accessible to the public as well as to its own Members, is further evinced by the fact that the Orders of the House for Printing have been in two distinct forms, the one directing the Printing in general terms, the other for the use of Members. Sometimes the general Printing has been negatived and the limited resolution adopted; and there are remarkable cases in which certain Papers having been directed in the first instance to be Printed for the use of Members, second Orders were made, after a short interval, for Printing the same Papers without any such restriction; thus clearly showing that the *publication* of Papers Ordered to be Printed was contemplated, unless special directions to the contrary were given.

Appx. (A.) No. 1, paragraphs 44 to 50.

Appx. No. 3, p. 78.

24. Your Committee find also that from the year 1691 the Printed Votes of this House have always been treated by the House of Lords as documents published by the authority of this House, and they are always referred to by their Lordships as the means of knowledge of any of the proceedings of this House of which it is deemed necessary to take notice. No instance has been found in which the Lords have adverted to the Journals; and although this House does not allow any reference to be made in Petitions to what passes in debate, or may be entered in the Journals, yet, consistently with the rules of the House, matter stated in the Printed Votes may be made the subject of petition and discussion.

Votes of this House treated by the House of Lords as authorized publications.

Appx. (A.) No. 1, par. 55 to 63.

25. The earliest instance upon record of the House of Lords treating the Printed Votes and Proceedings of this House as Publications put forth by authority, occurs in 1691, upon a Debate concerning the Regulations of the East India Company, when, on the 30th December, it was resolved, that the Printed Vote (of this House) then read was sufficient ground for that House (the Lords) to take notice of it to the House of Commons.

15 Lords' Journals, p. 10. A. D. 1691.

26. The publicity of printed Parliamentary Papers has not only been thus separately recognized by both Houses of Parliament, but has further received what amounts to the express sanction of the whole Legislature, by the exemption of such papers from postage. The title of the statute of the 42 Geo. 3, c. 63, is, "An Act to *authorize the sending and receiving* of letters and packets, *Votes and Proceedings in Parliament*, and printed newspapers, *by the Post, free from* the duty of *Postage*, by the Members of the two Houses of Parliament of the United Kingdom, and by certain public officers therein named, and *for reducing the Postage* on *such Votes, Proceedings* and newspapers *when sent by any other persons*."

27. With regard to the Publication of Papers by the House of Lords, Your Committee have inserted in the Appendix to this Report several examples, taken from the period immediately after the Revolution, of express Orders made by that House for printing *and publishing* various Resolutions and other Documents. These examples sufficiently prove that the House of Lords has, equally with this House, exercised the power of ordering the general publication of Papers printed by its directions.

Appx. (A.) No. 1, par. 98. 55, 64 to 77.

Practice as to Publication since the Order of August 1835.

28. Your Committee proceed to state the practice of this House in the circulation of its Reports and Papers *since the recent Order*, first remarking, that of late years the demand for Parliamentary Papers has greatly increased; the application for them to Members, and the obtaining the Speaker's authority, that the Member should be supplied with them, necessarily occasioned trouble, delay, and difficulty. Many persons interested in their contents were unknown to Members; and in populous places, more persons desired to obtain copies than were able to procure them; and although copies might always have been obtained by purchase at the Vote Office, yet that circumstance was not universally known, and single Papers could not be purchased, complete sets for the whole Session being alone disposed of.

Appx. No. 8, p. 79 to 84.

Appx. No. 4, p. 85, 86, 88, 90, 91.

Appx. No. 4. Extract 8, p. 94.

Com. Journ. vol. 90, p. 544. Appx. No. 4, p. 98.

29. The inadequacy of the system of publication, before described, attracted the attention of this House and led to the appointment of a Committee, which presented its Report on the 16th day of July 1835, recommending that the Sessional Papers of this House should be printed and sold by appointed persons, at the lowest price, under arrangements calculated to secure a speedy and economical distribution of the Parliamentary Proceedings. In pursuance of that Report, the House, on the 13th August 1835, Resolved, "that the Parliamentary Papers and Reports printed for the use of the House should be rendered *accessible to the public at the lowest price they can be furnished*, and that a sufficient number of extra copies should be printed for that purpose."

Ib. vol. 91, p. 16.

Appx. No. 4, p. 96.

30. In March 1836 a Committee was appointed, consisting of the Speaker and eight Members, "To assist him in all matters relating to the Printing executed by order of the House." At the commencement of the present Session a similar Committee was appointed, which has made various regulations respecting the printing and sale of the Votes and Proceedings, and fixed the price to be charged. Certain establishments have been appointed for the sale, under the superintendence of Messrs. Hansard, and a price is affixed, at one-third less than the cost at which the Reports or Papers can be produced; and by these arrangements, public economy and convenience have been greatly promoted. It ought here to be remarked, that the proceeds of the Sale are placed to the Public Account in diminution of the Expenses of the Printing.

App. No. 3, p. 80; and Appx. No. 4, p. 96.

Papers printed for the House not questioned in courts of law.

31. The public circulation of Papers printed by order of this House having thus been shown to have continued without interruption for nearly two centuries, Your Committee conceive it to be most material to remark, in the next place, that it appears to have been the generally received opinion, during the whole of that period, that legal proceedings could not be instituted for any thing contained in Papers so printed.

32. Your Committee have been led to the conclusion that such must have been the case by the fact that the prosecutions arising out of the publication of Dangerfield's Narrative, in 1684, are the only instances which Your Committee have been able to discover, before Mr. Stockdale's action, of any legal proceeding upon account of any publication *under the authority of the House*. The particulars of the prosecution of Sir William Williams in this case, to which Your Committee will again have occasion to advert, are stated in the Appendix, and are very important.

Appx. (B.) p. 34.

33. The absence of any other example of proceedings having been taken in a Court of Law upon Papers printed by order of the House, is the more important on adverting to the character of many of these papers, and the severity with which at a former period the offenders of the press were habitually treated.

treated. While the publication of Parliamentary Papers has prevailed, there have been contained among them Resolutions, Reports and Petitions, imputing misconduct to and reflecting in a high degree upon individuals in every rank of society. The inquiries prosecuted by the House, from the Revolution, to the present time, have been occasionally severe and searching, and full particulars of such Proceedings have been published. Some of the Papers published by the House of Lords have also strongly inculpated individuals. Upon some occasions of controversy between the two Houses, publications have been made by each severely reflecting upon the other.

34. In the Appendix will be found a List of Reports printed for this House, which will exclude any possible doubt that numerous prosecutions, civil and criminal, would have followed those publications, and necessarily have put a stop to them, unless an impression had universally prevailed that parties engaged in the publication were clothed with a Parliamentary protection. There will likewise be found some instances of an early date of Resolutions published by the Lords of a character to have challenged exception unless protected by Parliamentary Privilege. Appendix, No. 5, p. 97.

---

35. Your Committee having thus detailed the facts relating to the Publication of the Reports and Proceedings of Parliament, and having shown the uniform practice of nearly two centuries, which seems to Your Committee to prove that injurious reflections contained in any publications ordered by Parliament have never, up to the time of the recent trial of *Stockdale* v. *Hansard*, been regarded as affording ground for proceedings in a Court of Law, beg leave now to call the attention of the House to the results which will follow if a different principle is for the future to be established.

36. It will be observed, on reference to the extracts Your Committee have made from the proceedings in the case of *Stockdale* and *Hansard*, that the Lord Chief Justice has drawn a distinction between Papers merely written and printed for the use of the Members of the House and those which are published, admitting the protection of Parliamentary Privilege to extend to the former, though he has so decidedly declared it to be inapplicable to the latter. It might possibly be inferred, from the expressions made use of in the charge of the noble and learned Judge, that he meant to draw a further distinction between a publication by Sale or otherwise; but as in this instance the defendants were proved to have no interest whatever in the Sale, so that no improper motive or malice could be inferred from it, Your Committee apprehend that such could not have been his Lordship's view, since they believe it to be a well-ascertained principle in the Law of Libel, that it is the publication and the motive of the publisher (in general evidenced by the tendency of the publication) which constitute the offence, and that the manner in which such publication takes place is no otherwise material than as it may, in some cases, tend to establish the malicious intent of the party, or to increase the amount of damage. Apart from these considerations, they believe it has been repeatedly held that the gratuitous distribution of libels, or even the fact of putting into the post a letter containing libellous matter, is as much a publication as one which is effected by sale. Appendix, No. 1, p. 63. 2 Starkie Evidence, Tit. Libel, Publication, pp. 465-7.

37. It must therefore be assumed, that the real effect of the recent decision of the Lord Chief Justice would be to confine the protection of Parliamentary Privilege to Papers printed strictly for the use of Members, and to render any party publishing them, even though with the direct sanction of the House, liable to answer in a Court of Law for whatever they might contain of a libellous character; in which, if the proceedings were of a criminal

minal nature, even the truth of the matter published would furnish no defence.

38. Your Committee have already shown that, previous to the resumption of the Sale of Parliamentary Papers, in conformity with the Resolution of August 1835, the publication was very extensive. If, therefore, the principle laid down by the Lord Chief Justice be correct, it would not be sufficient to rescind this Resolution, the publication must be altogether abandoned; since the Speaker, by directing the distribution of Papers of this description according to the former practice, and Members, by communicating them to their constituents, would become subject to actions on the part of every person who considered himself reflected upon by anything they might happen to contain. Such being the case, Your Committee are of opinion that the establishment of this as a rule of law would be fatal to the proper exercise of its functions by the House. The very groundwork of all sound legislation is ample and correct information with regard to all abuses and defects of the existing laws and institutions of the country; but this information it would be absolutely impossible to obtain if the House were debarred from communicating, except to its own Members, the Papers which it is from time to time necessary to print, whenever they contained anything which in law would constitute a Libel. Your Committee need scarcely call the attention of the House to the fact that, if it were necessary to exclude all matter which might be held to be of a libellous character, these Papers would, in numberless instances, be altogether useless for the purposes for which they are intended. For example: the Committee appointed in the year 1832 to investigate the condition of the Slave population in the British Colonies, was under the absolute necessity, in order to perform the duty assigned to them, of receiving a large mass of evidence as to cases of alleged cruelty committed towards Slaves; this evidence, there can be no doubt, would have been regarded, if published in an unauthorized form, as affording good grounds for actions or prosecutions for libel to the parties to whom cruelty was imputed; yet, if its circulation had been confined to Members of the House, or if, in printing it, the names of those accused had been omitted, the object in view would not have been obtained. This object was to throw light on the effects of the institution of slavery, and to elicit from the conflicting statements of persons of opposite views and opinions the real facts which were to guide the judgment of the House, and the only mode by which this could be accomplished, and by which any security could be obtained for the correctness of that information upon which, in the following year, a most important Act of the Legislature was to be founded, was the publication of the evidence, in order that it might be subjected to the scrutiny of those who, if it were false, would be interested in disproving it. Yet, according to the rule which has now been laid down, the publication of this evidence being sufficient to justify legal proceedings by the very numerous persons whom it inculpated, all the important national advantages to be derived from such publication must necessarily have been abandoned.

39. Many similar examples might be brought forward; the Reports of the Committees of this House, and of the Commissioners who inquired into the state of the Municipal Corporations of England and of Ireland, those of the Charity Commissioners, and of the Commissioners for inquiring into the operation of the Poor Laws, in exposing the abuses which it was the object of the Legislature to correct, must unavoidably have contained a multitude of statements which, in unauthorised publications, would have been considered libellous; indeed, it is not too much to assert that perhaps the greater part of the Reports and Papers printed by the House would be found, if subjected to a

nice

nice and critical examination, to contain matter of a defamatory character; nay, in some cases, the same might be said of printed copies of Bills brought into the House, and which have ultimately passed into Acts of Parliament, as, for instance, the Bills for the Disfranchisement of Grampound and East Retford.

40. Your Committee hold it to be altogether needless to dwell further upon the utter impossibility of legislating with advantage which would result from depriving this House of the unrestricted power of communicating with the people whom it represents, and of collecting and diffusing information upon the various subjects which are brought under its consideration; but they think it right further to observe, that this is by no means the only difficulty which would arise from the recognition of the principle now contended for with regard to the Publication of Parliamentary Papers. This House is, in Parliamentary language, termed the Grand Inquest of the Nation; in this capacity, it is its duty to inquire into all wrongs and grievances of which either the people at large or any individuals may have reason to complain, and it has cognizance of all cases in which power has been abused by those to whom it has been by law entrusted. These important functions, it is obvious, could not be exercised if the House had no power to protect the publication as well of Petitions addressed to it, alleging criminality against any parties, as of the proceedings adopted with reference to such Petitions; without this power, it would have no means of investigating the truth of complaints brought before it, or of obtaining such redress as the several cases may require.

41. The great and public benefit thus demonstrated to arise from the possession of this power by Parliament, and the great and public injury which would arise from the absence of such power, would in themselves go far to prove the legality of the Publication. But the subject under consideration is of such importance, that Your Committee deem it necessary to offer some further observations upon the legal questions which it involves.

42. The first legal point for consideration is, how far the affirmance by Parliament of the Privilege which has been denounced will afford protection to those who may, under the sanction of this House, conduct the Sale of such Publications as may be ordered, and to whom the truth of the matter so published will furnish no defence against a criminal prosecution; or, in other words, whether this House has the exclusive jurisdiction to decide upon the existence and extent of its own Privileges. But before entering upon the consideration of that subject, the Committee beg to refer to the case of *The King* v. *Wright*, showing what has been, by high judicial authority, considered the legal character of the Publication of Proceedings in Parliament reflecting upon individuals, even without authority or sanction.

43. Mr. Horne Tooke moved for a criminal information against the defendant for the republication of a Report made by a Committee of Secrecy, which had been ordered to be printed *for the use of the Members*, imputing treasonable intentions to him, in reference to political conduct, for which he had been tried and acquitted. Lord KENYON stated that it was impossible for the court to admit that the proceeding of either House of Parliament was a Libel; that the Report having been adopted by the House at large, was a proceeding of those who by the constitution were the guardians of the liberty of the subject, and that it could not be said that any part of that proceeding was *a Libel*. Mr. Justice LAWRENCE said it was of advantage to the public, and even to the legislative bodies, that true accounts of their proceedings should be generally circulated, and they would be deprived of that advantage if no person could publish their proceedings without being in danger of being punished as a libeller; though therefore the defendant was not *authorised by the House of Commons*, yet as he only published a true copy of it, the rule (praying for the criminal information) ought to be discharged.

House of Commons in matters of Privilege represent the whole Parliament.

44. The importance of that branch of the *lex terræ* which embraces the Law and Privilege of Parliament is commensurate with the constitutional value of Parliament itself, as its independence, and the judicious and effective use of that independence, must arise out of the Privileges it possesses, and it becomes important here to note that these Privileges are not the attributes of either House individually, but of the whole Parliament, and that however the jurisdiction of the High Court of Parliament may be exercised by one or the other of its different branches, in the name, and by the authority, of the whole, yet that this House forms a constituent part of, and is presumed to be present in, that Supreme Court, the highest judicature known to the nation,* and cannot, in the essence of its authority and privilege, be separated from it. The judicial authority of that Supreme Court, it is true, is administered by the House of Lords; but it is nevertheless the High Court of Parliament, and in its name and under its sanction that the judgment is pronounced.†

45. The constitution of Parliament, previously to the separation of the Two Houses, and the jurisdiction and authority that devolved upon each at that time, has been the subject of so much learned argument, and has so long been taken to be a matter beyond dispute, that Your Committee only deem it

State Trials, vol. 13, p. 1380.
necessary to refer to Sir Robert Atkyns' argument in the case of Sir William Williams, and the authorities therein cited, and Lord Ellenborough's judgment

14 East, 136-7.
in *Burdett* v. *Abbot*, as conclusive in showing that the Privilege of each House respectively includes the collective Privilege of Parliament.

46. In 34 Hen. 8. (1543), the Commons complained to the King and the

App. (B.) p. 49.
Lords, of a Breach of Privilege, by arresting one Ferrers, a Member; and upon that occasion the King expressed himself to the following purport: "And

1 Hatsell, p. 57.
further, *we be informed by our Judges*, that we at no time stand so highly in our Estate Royal, as in the time of Parliament; wherein we as Head, and you as Members, are conjoined and knit together into one body politic; so as whatsoever offence or injury (during that time) is offered to the meanest Member of the House, is to be judged as done against our Person and the whole Court of Parliament; which prerogative of the Court is so great (as our learned counsel informeth us) as all acts and processes coming out of any other inferior courts, must for the time cease and give place to the highest."

47. As the Privilege of each House respectively is derived from and identified with the collective Privilege of Parliament, it becomes essential to bear in mind the basis upon which it rests; that basis Your Committee hold to be the *protection of the public interests as connected with the discharge of the duties and the maintenance of the authority with which Parliament is for public purposes invested.* The precise limits of Parliamentary Privilege cannot be defined, because the emergencies which may call for its exercise cannot be foreseen. In the same manner a Court of Law does not *à priori* define a contempt. The constitutional limit of Parliamentary Privilege is determined by the principle, that that only is a legitimate Privilege which has for its object either the upholding of the authority essential to the due exercise of Parliamentary functions, or to the effective discharge, for the common good, of the duties which those functions involve. Neither the public safety nor the public service recognizes any claim of Privilege beyond the limit of this principle. And Your Committee consider that no Privilege of Parliament can, in its exercise, be more beneficial than that under which it gives

* Sir Matthew Hale's Treatise upon the Jurisdiction of the House of Lords will be found to contain the whole learning upon the subject.

† For the form of the judgment upon a Writ of Error in Parliament, vide Tidd's App. p. 690.

gives to the people the result of its public inquiries, connected with the conduct of public men, and the management, good or bad, of public institutions. The numerous Commissions and Inquiries which have been prosecuted have been directed to this end.

48. The above considerations would seem sufficient to establish the existence of the Privilege adverted to, but they derive additional weight from the existence of the long Parliamentary usage, which has been shown from 1641 to the present time without objection or complaint, not exercised *sub silentio*, but, on the contrary, under circumstances calculated to excite resistance if that right had been doubted. The case of *The King* v. *Williams* is the only exception. The time of its decision, and the manner in which it was conducted, have caused it to be considered as of no authority, and it is only worthy of reference because it led to proceedings which Your Committee think bear decisively upon the present question*.

App. (A.) and App. No. 3.

App. (B.)

49. In that case an attempt was made to establish the doctrine laid down in *Stockdale* v. *Hansard*, viz. that the Officers of this House were amenable for the contents of publications issued by its order; and attention was then called to the subject in a remarkable manner; the judgment pronounced by the Court of King's Bench, on that occasion, was condemned in a distinct Resolution of this House as illegal and against the freedom of Parliament,† and it was also in effect denounced in the Bill of Rights as subversive of the laws and liberties of the kingdom: these circumstances and the subsequent undisturbed continuance of publication, in conformity with the Privilege asserted, appear to Your Committee to furnish decisive evidence in maintenance of the right of Parliament to issue, at its discretion, publications respecting matters coming before it connected with the public interest. Nothing has since occurred, that Your Committee can discover, to justify any doubt as to the legitimate existence and extent of that right.

Rep. 1771. App. (B.)

50. The Committee cannot forbear to recur to the extraordinary periods of our history through which the precedents prevail, and to remark, that the abuse of the Privilege during the Long Parliament could not fail to have arrested attention when the constitutional powers of the State were restored, and that the undeviating adherence to the Privilege, through the reign of Charles II. proves that the restored Government regarded it as inseparable from the Parliamentary trust. And further, that the strong complaint urged by this House immediately after the Revolution, of the attempt made to destroy it in the prosecution of Sir William Williams, and the distinct re-assertion

---

* The particulars of this Case, with the observations of Your Committee, will be found in the Appendix. Upon being cited to the Court of King's Bench, in *Rex* v. *Wright*, 8 Term Rep., Lord Kenyon remarked, "It was a case that had happened in the worst of times;" and Mr. J. Grose observed that this case "had been said by a great authority to be a disgrace to the country."

† The judgment was pronounced in the year 1686; and in the year 1689 the Commons passed the following Resolution: "*That the judgment given in the Court of King's Bench, against W. Williams, Esq., Speaker of the House of Commons, for matters done by order of the House of Commons and as Speaker thereof, was an illegal judgment, and against the freedom of Parliament;*" and it was further resolved, "*that a Bill be brought in to reverse the said judgment.*" A Bill was accordingly brought in in the year 1689; its object was to reverse the judgment, and to procure to Sir W. Williams a restitution of the damages which had been recovered from him. It proceeded through certain stages, but did not pass. Two Bills were subsequently brought in for the same purpose in 1690 and 1695, which passed the Commons, and were read twice in the House of Lords; but what ultimately became of them cannot be traced.

See App. (B.) pp. 64 to 68.

The reasons why these Bills did not pass do not appear upon any authority; but their failure is supposed to have been occasioned by the difficulty of determining upon whom the charge of reimbursing the Speaker should be laid. By the Bills, it was proposed that the Attorney-General, who instituted the prosecution, should repay the money, and he was heard at the Bar by his Counsel against the Bill; but it seems clear that the desire of Parliament to procure a reconsideration was the cause why the Bills to reverse the judgment did not pass.

tion of it, accompanied by a correspondent usage of nearly a century and a half, affirm it by evidence too conclusive to admit any reasonable ground of contest.

Exclusive jurisdiction in matter of Privilege.

51. Although each House is separately vested with all the Privileges that belong to the Parliament as a body, it yet remains to be considered whether Parliament possesses *exclusive* authority to determine upon the extent of these Privileges, or whether the Courts of Law have a jurisdiction enabling them to review and control the decisions of Parliament upon the subject.

52. In considering the relative jurisdiction of Parliament and of the Courts of Law, it will be material to keep in remembrance the earlier course of Parliament, when the King as Head and the three Estates of the Realm as Members of the Parliament, sat together to discuss the affairs of the Nation, to make Laws, and to *review the decisions of inferior courts*, and to this High Court of Parliament those tribunals resorted for advice in cases involving more than ordinary difficulty. We may readily assume that this Highest Court of the Nation would not permit its decisions, in respect of its own jurisdiction, to be questioned or reviewed by Judges subordinate in station, over whom they were in the course of exercising a supreme control, and who, being created by, and holding their offices at the pleasure of the Crown, might be swayed by an adverse influence.

53. If the Courts at Westminster have authority to determine upon the Privileges of Parliament, the same power is incident to the County Court and courts of inferior jurisdiction. If the Court of King's Bench were competent to have decided against the power of this House, in the action of trespass in the case of *Burdett* v. *Abbot*, the County Court of Middlesex would have possessed equal authority had the damages been laid under 40 *s.*, and the formal words "with force and arms" been omitted; in both Courts the question would have been the same, whether the Speaker's warrant justified the alleged trespass and imprisonment? When the comparative importance and authority of the High Court of Parliament, and the Sheriff's Tourn and County Court be considered, and the decisive and summary manner in which Parliament had been accustomed to vindicate its authority against those who impugned it, is adverted to, the House will judge whether any reasonable doubt can be entertained as to the ancient state of the law.

54. It would be easy to adduce ample proof from history that the Privileges of Parliament have formed a strong, and in many instances, the only barrier against the encroachments of Royal Power; but Your Committee are of opinion that the constitutional freedom of the subject could not have been so defended, had those Privileges been subject to be overruled by Judges holding their situation, as they then did, at the pleasure of the Crown, and having therefore the strongest personal interest in keeping in favour with the Court. A very cursory acquaintance with the legal history of the country, and with the decisions of the Courts of Law on questions involving the power and interests of the Crown, will be sufficient to show how very slight a vestige, either of parliamentary independence, or of popular liberty, would have survived to the present day, if those Courts had possessed and exercised such paramount jurisdiction.

55. If, as is the Opinion of Your Committee, the Privileges of Parliament are held in trust for the benefit of the people, it becomes most important to ascertain where the sacred duty of protecting and maintaining them is constitutionally deposited.

56. If

56. If deposited, as Your Committee think this duty cannot but be, in Parliament, it must have arisen from the constitutional attributes of that assembly, representing, and, in contemplation of law, including the whole body of the People; which consideration appears to furnish the most valid guarantee for the due exercise of the Privileges of Parliament, and the best security against their perversion. Under such circumstances, a surrender of its authority would be a dereliction of trust; and practically surrendered it would be, if a Court of Law were suffered to control its jurisdiction, and by controlling to defeat it.

57. The instant these Privileges are subject to any other jurisdiction than that of Parliament, all security for their existence is at an end; a new element of power is introduced into the State, and the Legislative Assembly of the Nation is no longer supreme.

58. The exclusive jurisdiction of Parliament to decide upon matters of Privilege was recognized by the Common Law tribunals at a very early period, and all power repudiated by those Courts to review or examine into the legality of the decisions of Parliament in that respect, when the question of Privilege should come *directly* into decision; but it has been said that when the question of Privilege arises *incidentally*, the Courts, of necessity, must decide upon it. The decisions repudiating the direct jurisdiction are of early date, numerous and consistent, while those which treat of the power of the Courts to decide incidentally upon Privilege fail in developing any principle by which the supposed extent of that power can be ascertained. Your Committee have, in the Appendix, referred to the leading authorities upon the subject; and they are fully sufficient to show that the claim of jurisdiction by the Courts is limited to this extent.

59. Your Committee have not been able to discover any satisfactory rule or test by which to ascertain in all cases whether the question of Privilege would be deemed to arise *directly* or *incidentally*; there are many cases which might be decisively placed in the one class or the other, but there may be also very many which cannot be so assigned.

60. Your Committee are of opinion that the Courts have no jurisdiction to decide upon Privilege, *either directly or incidentally*, in any sense inconsistent with the independence and exclusive jurisdiction of Parliament. If such a jurisdiction did exist of deciding *incidentally* upon Privilege, uncontrolled by Parliament, it would lead to proceedings as incongruous, and as effectually destructive of the independence of Parliament as if the *direct* jurisdiction existed; a consequence which, together with the extreme uncertainty of the extent of the rule, makes it indispensably necessary that it should be investigated.

61. The decision in Messrs. Hansard's case, which has created the necessity for this inquiry, shows the peril in which Privilege would be placed under even this *incidental* jurisdiction. It was held in *Burdett* v. *Abbot*, that the defence being founded upon the Order of the House to do the act complained of, raised the question of Privilege *directly*, and that the Court could not investigate the legality of that Order; the defence of Messrs. Hansard was also founded upon the Order of the House. Your Committee are unable to distinguish in principle between the two cases; but it being admitted law in all Courts, that there is no *direct* jurisdiction over Privilege out of Parliament, it must be supposed that the Privilege was deemed in this case to arise *incidentally*; and if that view be correct, it will follow that persons acting under the Orders of the House might be subjected to large damages, or indeed to imprisonment, by a sentence in a criminal prosecution under this *incidental* jurisdiction.

62. The nature and consequence of the jurisdiction thus claimed, will be best appreciated by examining some of the consequences to which it may lead. Applications to be discharged from commitments by Parliament, and actions brought by persons imprisoned under warrants granted by The Speaker of this House, are proceedings held to raise the question of Privilege *directly*, and, therefore, not examinable by Courts of Law, who can afford no relief in such cases, even supposing the case of a commitment by the House of Lords for a fine, however large, or that of an imprisonment, by either House. But it is said that the Privileges of Parliament may be brought *incidentally* into judgment in those Courts, and that then they may be overruled. But if the party be committed by Parliament for so bringing its Privileges under the consideration of the inferior tribunal, though it should appear upon the face of the warrant that the commitment was founded solely upon that ground, the Court nevertheless could give no relief, nor could those who enforced the imprisonment be in any manner rendered amenable. Suppose the commitment to be by the House of Lords, and the Privilege brought into question *incidentally*, and *overruled*, and a writ of error then brought in Parliament, by that course the question of Privilege would come back to the same jurisdiction *which had originally decided upon it*; and had the commitment been made by *this* House, the effect would be that its Privileges, and consequently its independence, would become subject to the decision of the other House of Parliament; thus all the evils consequent on a direct jurisdiction would equally result from incidental decisions. The case of *The Queen* v. *Patey* is strikingly illustrative of the present subject. It arose out of the decision in the case of *Ashby* v. *White*, which was an action against the returning officer of the borough of Aylesbury, for rejecting the plaintiff's vote at an election. The defendant insisted that the right to vote was matter for the decision of this House alone, and that the Courts of Law could not entertain the question; and, therefore, that no action could be maintained. Three of the Judges of the Court of King's Bench held the action not to be maintainable; Lord Chief Justice Holt held the contrary. Judgment was of course entered for the defendant, upon which a writ of error was brought in Parliament. The Judges were there called upon for their opinion; three Judges agreed with Lord Holt for the plaintiff, two concurred with the three Judges of the King's Bench in favour of the defendant. Upon this the House of Lords, on a division of 50 against 16, reversed the judgment of the Court of King's Bench, and by this reversal asserted and in effect exercised a jurisdiction over the rights of voting for *Members of this House*, which had (pending the proceedings) resolved, That the decision of the right to Vote at an Election for a Member of this House by *any other* tribunal, was a *Breach of its Privileges*.

App. (A.) Par. 88. Hatsell, vol. 3, p. 247.

63. After the decision of the House of Lords, *Patey* and several other persons brought similar actions, upon which they were summoned to the Bar of this House, and committed for the Breach of Privilege in bringing such actions, the warrants upon the face of them stating the whole cause of commitment. Writs of Habeas Corpus were obtained from the King's Bench, and the case was argued before the twelve Judges; eleven of them held that the Court had no power to examine the question of Privilege, as the House had decided it, and that the parties could not be discharged. Lord Holt was of a contrary opinion. A very unusual expedient was in this case adopted to draw the Privilege of *this* House still further under the consideration of the Lords. The Queen was prayed to grant a writ of error, in order to bring the decision of the Judges under the review of the Lords. Against this the Commons protested, and the Lords, who were to decide upon that writ of error, did not wait until it should come judicially before them, but addressed the Queen, praying

praying for the immediate issuing of the writ of error, and very severely animadverted on this House, and ordered the Address *to be published*. This House indicated an intention to vindicate its Privileges, when a course was taken similar to that which has been pursued on other occasions when the House has been called upon to maintain its Privilege, namely, a dissolution of Parliament. Which dissolution had the effect of discharging the parties who had been committed, and the discussion was not revived.

64. The decision in *Burdett* v. *Abbot* is in conformity with the opinion of the eleven Judges in *Paty*'s case, who held the Order of this House conclusive.

65. The present case, in which the Privilege of the House to make its proceedings public has been denied, and *Ashby* v. *White*, in which the House of Lords exercised the power of determining on the right of voting, will sufficiently illustrate the effect of this alleged *incidental* jurisdiction upon the independence and authority of the House, according to the view which has been taken of it. But Your Committee are impressed with the opinion that the effect of this incidental jurisdiction has been the subject of some misapprehension, and that it will not be found to exist to an extent incompatible with the independence and paramount authority of Parliament.

66. There are many subjects over which particular courts have an exclusive jurisdiction, and the judgments of which are therefore conclusive even upon the superior courts, whilst the paramount authority of Parliament over the Courts of Law must never be forgotten. Where a cause is depending which *incidentally* involves a matter subject to an *exclusive jurisdiction* which has *not pronounced upon it*, the Court where the cause is so depending is compelled to decide the incidental question in order to determine such cause; but in so deciding, the Court does not overrule the authority or judgment of the exclusive jurisdiction. Yet in cases of Privilege it seems to be assumed by some that the question arising incidentally would give authority to overrule the judgment of Parliament, which is admitted to be a Court having a competent and exclusive jurisdiction; but except in the case of *Brayon* v. *Evelyn*, it is nowhere stated that a Resolution of Parliament would not be conclusive upon a question of Privilege, whether such question arose directly or incidentally; and Your Committee apprehend that such a Resolution must be so treated to be consistent either with the principles applied to other exclusive jurisdictions, or the doctrines applied by the Courts to Parliament itself. The duty of Courts to decide all questions which arise incidentally is quite consistent with the judgments of Courts of competent and exclusive jurisdiction being, when proved, conclusive upon the matter expressly decided.

Appendix (A.) p. 87, par. 109.

67. This House has constantly asserted and frequently exercised its highest powers in maintaining an exclusive jurisdiction; of this the case of *The Queen* v. *Paty* furnishes a striking example; and it might have been expected that the judgment of the eleven Judges, and its subsequent confirmation by every succeeding Judge, that the adjudication of the House was *conclusive*, would have put an end to the question.

68. Your Committee beg to refer to the Report of the Committee appointed to report upon the causes of the duration of the Trial of Warren Hastings.

40 Com. Jour. p. 384. Parl. Hist. vol. 31, p. 287.

---

69. Your Committee having considered the subject of Parliamentary Privilege, and the Jurisdiction of this House to determine the extent of its own Privileges, submit, as their opinion, that by the Law and Usage of Parliament,

Parliament, the House of Commons does possess an *exclusive* Jurisdiction, and that it is a breach of its Privileges to bring them into discussion for decision before any other tribunal *directly* or *incidentally*, and that such breach of Privilege subjects the parties to punishment by this House.

70. Your Committee are of opinion, That the long usage which has pre-
App. (B.) p. 54. vailed, and the distinct Resolution of this House in *The King* v. *Williams*, and the public proceedings which afterwards followed in that case, and the recent
90 Com. Jour. p. 544, and App. No. 4, p. 98. Orders of the House for Printing its proceedings, sufficiently establish and notify the Privilege in question; and that the action brought by Mr. Stockdale against Messrs. Hansard was a breach of the Privileges of this House.

71. It would add unnecessarily to the length of this Report to detail all the
Reports of the H. C. 1810, (354) vol. 2, p. 315. authorities upon which this opinion is formed. The First Report presented in the year 1810 by the Select Committee on the Proceedings relative to Sir Francis Burdett, furnishes all that is material on the subject, and the conclusion
Hansard, vol. 1, p. 181. which that Committee came to was, that the actions brought against The Speaker and the Serjeant for acts done in obedience to the Orders of the House were in *Breach of its Privileges*. Your Committee beg leave also to refer to the Second Report made by that Committee, in which numerous authorities are brought together on the same subject.

72. Attending to the law laid down in the action against Messrs. Hansard, it becomes most material to consider, whether to permit the decision to pass unnoticed would not be in effect to recognise it, and virtually to suffer one of the most important functions of this House, that of inquiring into public abuses, to be defeated, and the right of the public to information as to the result of such inquiries to be put an end to. And above all, whether, if the assumption of the jurisdiction to decide upon the existence and extent of Privilege were acquiesced in, the Supremacy and Independence of Parliament would not be thereby superseded.

73. It does not appear to Your Committee that any further proceedings should take place in the cause of *Stockdale* v. *Hansard*. The action was brought by the plaintiff *in formâ pauperis*. He has obtained a verdict against the defendant upon the issue of *not guilty*, which, in effect, negatived the existence of the Privilege, but the defendant has obtained a verdict upon the second issue, under which the publication was *justified* upon the ground that it was *true*, which latter issue furnishes a full defence to the action; the plaintiff has, consequently, no interest in proceeding further, and the House is not therefore called upon to take any step for the future protection of Messrs. Hansard in relation to the cause; the plaintiff having sued *in formâ pauperis*, the defendant will not recover his costs; so that neither party has any interest in taking any further step. In ordinary cases, the misdirection of the Judge affords ground for an application for a new trial. In the present case, the defendant having succeeded, no reason existed for any such application, except for the mere purpose of bringing the law laid down at Nisi Prius under the review of the Court; but Your Committee are of opinion, that any such application to the Court, under the sanction of this House, would have been inconsistent with its dignity and subversive of its authority.

74. It appears to Your Committee essential that all doubt on the question of Privilege, in the present case, should be set at rest, it being still competent to Mr. Stockdale to prefer an indictment against the Messrs. Hansard for the same Publication, in which the truth would furnish the latter with no defence; and equally open to every individual who may conceive himself directly or incidentally implicated in any Report which may have been published under the Authority of this House, to prosecute civilly or criminally

minally either Messrs. Hansard or any other Officer (including The Speaker) of the House, who may have ordered or may otherwise have been concerned in causing such publication, and in the event of criminal proceedings being resorted to, the truth of the matter would, as already observed, furnish no defence.

75. It seems most important that the Proceedings of Parliament upon the subject of Privilege should be uniform; submission to the Courts of Law upon some occasions, and resistance upon others, begets an impression in the public mind that Parliament itself wavers, and has no settled conviction on the subject of its Privileges; an impression which is not justified, and ought not to prevail.

76. With regard to the Petition of James Hansard and Luke G. Hansard, referred to Your Committee, they find that those persons have acted in strict obedience to the Orders of the House in selling the Report in question, and became subject to the proceeding which has been instituted against them solely in consequence thereof, and have thereby been subjected to considerable expense, for which they ought to be reimbursed. Your Committee feel it proper to add, that the direction of the Lord Chief Justice to the jury was pronounced under circumstances which preclude all supposition of an intentional violation of the Privileges of the House.

---

77. Upon the whole matter referred to Your Committee, they report as their opinion, That the power of publishing such of its Reports, Votes and Proceedings as it shall deem necessary or conducive to the public interests, is an essential incident to the constitutional functions of Parliament, more especially of this House, as the representative portion of it:

78. That by the Law and Privilege of Parliament, this House has the sole and exclusive jurisdiction to determine upon the existence and extent of its Privileges, and that the institution or prosecution of any action, suit or other proceeding for the purpose of bringing them into discussion or decision before any court or tribunal elsewhere than in Parliament, is a high breach of such Privilege, and renders all parties concerned therein amenable to its just displeasure, and to the punishment consequent thereon:

79. That for any court or tribunal to assume to decide upon matters of Privilege inconsistent with the determination of either House of Parliament thereon, is contrary to the law of Parliament, and is a breach and contempt of the Privileges of Parliament.

---

80. In concluding their Report, Your Committee feel it incumbent upon them to observe that, although they have expressed a decided opinion that it is absolutely essential to the effective discharge of the most important functions of the House of Commons, that the Privilege of Publication should exist without restriction, and that the authority to determine the extent of that Privilege and the occasion for exercising it should rest exclusively with Parliament, they are not insensible to the evil which may arise from an incautious printing of Parliamentary Documents, in cases wherein the character of individuals is involved, and wherein no public necessity calls for publication, or no opportunity is afforded to the party affected to give an immediate answer to the inculpation. Your Committee are aware that, without the previous sanction of this House, no publication of its Proceedings can be privileged; and that all presumption, therefore, of malicious motives is excluded; neither

have they the slightest doubt that if the attention of Parliament were directed to each individual case, ample precautions would be taken against the infliction of unnecessary pain, and still more against the possible case that the Privilege of Parliament may be abused for the mere gratification of resentments connected with personal or party differences. But, amidst the pressure of the important and multifarious business which occupy its attention, it is impossible to exercise, on all occasions, that precautionary vigilance which might effectually guard against the evil to which we have thus adverted. Much, therefore, must depend upon the discretion, and sense of justice of individual Members respecting the presentation and printing of Petitions, and of the Chairmen and Members of Committees of Inquiry, in respect to the prosecution of their inquiries, and particularly in respect to the printing of the evidence which may affect private character, until the opportunity be given of rebutting it. To prescribe any positive rule upon such a subject, is manifestly impossible. The invariable adherence to such a rule might protect public delinquents from a disclosure of their misconduct, or prevent the notoriety of facts important to the ends for which inquiry was instituted. It appears, however, to Your Committee (and they think that the practical experience of Members will support the conclusion to which they have come) that it would not be difficult, on a mature consideration of each case wherein the exercise of a discretion may be called for, so to apply it, in the great majority of instances, as completely to reconcile all proper regard for the character and feelings of individuals with the faithful and effectual discharge of public functions. The more essential the Privilege the more urgent the necessity for an exclusive and unfettered authority in deciding upon the exercise and the limits of it, the more important and the more becoming is it to take as much precaution as possible against the infliction of individual injury or unnecessary pain to private feelings.

8 May 1837.

APPENDIX

TO THE

REPORT.

—(A.)—

ORDERS and PROCEEDINGS of the Two Houses of Parliament relating to the PUBLICATION of PARLIAMENTARY REPORTS and PAPERS; and Review of the LEGAL AUTHORITIES upon the Jurisdiction of Parliament on Matters of PRIVILEGE.

No. 1.

PRINTING.

1. THE earliest entry in the Journals, relating to the printing of Parliamentary Papers, is on the 30th July 1641. At this date the House adopted certain Resolutions, and ordered they should be printed. 2 Com. Journ. 230.

2. The form of the entry is, "That these Votes be printed and attested under the clerk's hand."

3. This is the first instance that can be discovered of any Parliamentary Proceedings being denominated *Votes*.

4. In the following year, 1642, the House appointed a Committee to consider, among other things, "the best way of divulging, dispersing and publishing the Orders and Votes, and also the Declarations of the House, through the Kingdom, and of the well and true printing of them." Ib. p. 604. Dated, 4 June.

5. On the 9th day of June the Committee made a Report, when certain Papers were ordered to be printed, the number of copies of each being specified, and varying from 4,000 to 9,000. Ib. p. 618.

6. The above instances refer to the printing of *particular Papers* only.

7. In the second Parliament after the Restoration (being the first after the Convention Parliament) it is ordered, that none of the Proceedings of this House be Printed without the Order of this House. 13 C. 2. 14 May, 1661. 8 Com. Journ. 259.

8. The first *general* Resolution for printing the *Votes* is on the 30th October 1680; it is in these words:

9. "Resolved,—That the Votes of the House be printed, being first perused and signed by Mr. Speaker, and that Mr. Speaker nominate and appoint the person to print the same." 9 Com. Journ. p. 643.

10. In 1680-81 (24th March) the House resolved, "That the Votes *and Proceedings* of this House be printed, and that the care of the printing thereof, and the appointment of the Printer, be committed to Mr. Speaker." Ibid. p. 708.

11. From this time (1681) to the present, a Resolution to the same import has been adopted at the commencement of every Session; and the following sentence is often found added to such order, "That no person but such as he (The Speaker) shall appoint do presume to print the same." Pursuant to this Order, The Speaker appoints the Printer, and the first Vote Paper of the Session contains the above Resolution and Appointment, to the following purport: 10 Com. Journ. p. 252.

12. "By virtue of an Order made this day, I do appoint *A. B.* and *C. D.* to print the Votes and Proceedings of this House. *E. F.*, Speaker."

13. Under the authority of this Resolution and Appointment, the *Proceedings* have been Printed, consisting of Votes, Orders, Resolutions and Petitions: *Reports* and other Papers have been printed under specific Resolutions.

14. The only period during which the General Order for Printing the *Votes and Proceedings* of the House was suspended, was in the year 1702, when the House of Commons, on the 25th day of February, ordered, "That the Order 14 Com. Journ. p. 168.

Appendix —(A.)—

Order of the 26th October last (the ordinary Sessional Order before referred to) for Printing the Votes, be discharged." Upon which Order appears the following entry:

15. "The House finding the great inconveniences that have attended the Printing of the Votes,

16. "Resolved,—That it be a Standing Order of the House, that no Votes of the House shall be Printed *without the particular orders of the House.*

17. "Resolved,—That the Votes and Proceedings of the House be not published by the Clerks or any other persons whatsoever."

18. These Resolutions appear to have been occasioned by the House of Lords having endeavoured to anticipate an Address which had been voted to the Queen in that year by the Commons, to remove the Bishop of Worcester from the office of Almoner.

19. In the following Session, on the 23d day of November 1703, the House resumed the former practice and ordered, "That all the Votes of the House be Printed, being first perused, and that no other person do presume to print the same but such as shall be appointed.

14 Com. Journ. p. 731.

20. "Ordered,—That Mr. Speaker do peruse and appoint the Printing the Orders of this House."

21. From the year 1641, when printing was first adopted in the House, down to the present time, the printing of *specific Papers and Proceedings,* under express Resolutions of the House, appears to have been constantly practised, and there are frequent instances in 1702 and 1703, during the period when the general order for printing the *Votes and Proceedings* was suspended.

22. The Parliamentary Papers printed under these particular Resolutions consisted of the Journals, Bills before the House, Reports, Evidence taken before the House and Committees, and Commercial and Revenue Accounts and Returns.

23. From the above extracts, it appears that the practice of *Printing* the Votes and Proceedings of the House, and Parliamentary Papers, commenced in 1641, and has continued to the present time.

No. 2.

PUBLICATION.

See Sherwin S. O. Collection, in the Library of the House of Com. vol. 76. 78. and 8 Com. Jour. p. 6 to 134.

24. Among the tracts in the old library of the British Museum, forming part of the collection called "The King's Pamphlets," are to be found the Resolutions and Proceedings of the House of Commons, in 1660, relating to the Restoration of Charles the Second, and which were published by order of the House.

25. Afterwards the Commons having sent up an order to the Lords for burning the solemn League and Covenant, the Lords concurred in such order, and sent a message to the Commons to that effect, and it was

21 May. Ib. p. 258.

26. "Ordered,—That this Order be forthwith *printed and published.*"

A.D. 1661. 8 Com. Jour. p. 279.

27. On the 22d *June,* 13 C. 2, the King having sent a letter to The Speaker, Members were appointed to convey the thanks of the House to his Majesty, and they were "also to desire his Majesty's leave for printing of his letter."

Ib. 299.

28. On Friday, the 12*th of July,* in the same year, a Committee was appointed to inquire touching the authors, &c. of a seditious paper, entitled "Summary Reasons, &c."

Ib. 301.

29. On the following Monday, the 15*th July,* the Committee made their Report; whereupon Mr. *Prynne* confessed himself the author; he was ordered to withdraw, and after a debate the House resolved that the said paper was "an illegal, false, scandalous and seditious pamphlet." And they resolved that Mr. Prynne should be called in and reprehended: he was so accordingly; and "with much ingenuity and reverence to the House," he declared his submission, &c.; whereupon the following entry occurs:

30. "Resolved, upon the question,—That this House being well satisfied with the demeanor and acknowledgment of Mr. Prynne, doth remit his offence."

31. "Ordered,—That these Votes and Proceedings be forthwith *printed and published.*"

32. On

32. On 13th May 1662, 14 Car. 2, certain presentations, &c. concerning ecclesiastical livings, &c. having been made to the House, and certain Orders having been made thereupon; it is further "Ordered these Votes *be printed and published, that all persons concerned may take notice thereof.*" Appendix —(A.)—

33. Order, 5 June 1663 (15 C. 2,) "That none of the Votes, Orders or Proceedings of this House be put in print or published, without the especial order and leave of this House." 8 Com. Journ. 499.

34. There are likewise some most important documents relative to the period after the Restoration, and before the accession of James II. in Mr. C. W. Williams Wynn's volume, entitled "Votes and Proceedings of the Two last Parliaments, in 1680 and 1681;" and among them are the Votes of the Parliament held at Oxford in the year 1680. The Paper marked No. 4, contains an Order (under the date March 24th) for printing the Examination relative to an alleged Popish Plot; Mr. Kunbolt was appointed Printer for that purpose, and the Examination appears to have been *sold* at his shop.

35. In Nos. 13, 16 and 56 in that volume, which refer to the dates of November 16 and 19, 1680, and 10th of January 1681, it is stated, by way of advertisement, that certain Informations relative to Dangerfield's Narrative of the plot, are printed according to the Order of the House. This Narrative, as the House is aware, imputed to the then Duke of York a participation in the celebrated Meal-tub Plot: and it seems that the publication referred to in the advertisement, or some other relating to the plot here mentioned, was prepared under the immediate authority of the House; it being stated in an entry in the 9th volume of the Journals, under the date of the 20th November 1680, that Mr. Treby acquainted the House that, pursuant to the Order of the House, he had prepared an abstract in writing of the several letters and papers in his custody relating to the Popish Plot; whereupon it was ordered that the said letters and papers be printed, and it was recommended to Mr. Treby to take care therein. 2. G. Collection, vol. 76–81. Dangerfield's Narrative. ib. 76. 9 Com. Jour. p. 658.

36. In the year 1702 (1 Anne) a difference having arisen between the two Houses, concerning a Bill brought in by the Commons for *preventing occasional Conformity*, and also on the subject of the Public Accounts, after warm debates and several conferences, which led to no result, both Houses *published* their proceedings, by way of appeal to the Nation.* Bill to prevent occasional Conformity.

37. The Resolution on the part of the Commons is to the following tenor:

38. "Ordered,—That the Bill, intituled, An Act for preventing occasional Conformity, with the Amendments made by the Lords, and the Amendments made by this House to those Amendments, and the Reports of the several conferences, and of the free conference relating thereunto, and the proceedings thereupon, be *printed*: 27 February. 14 Com. Journ. p. 209.

39. "Ordered,—That Mr. Speaker do examine the said Bill, Amendments, Reports and Proceedings, and appoint the Printer thereof:

* * * * * * *

40. "Ordered,—That the Lords' Journals be inspected with relation to the Bill for preventing occasional Conformity, and that the same be printed, with the proceedings of this House in relation thereunto."

41. On Saturday, the 27th February, there is the following entry in the Journal of the House, on the subject of the Public Accounts: Public Accounts, 1702.

42. "Ordered,—That the Report of the Conferences and free Conference relating to the Message from the Lords the 4th instant, touching the Commissioners of Accounts, and the proceedings relating thereunto, be printed: 14 Com. Jour. p. 308.

43. "Ordered,—That Mr. Speaker do examine the said Reports and Proceedings, and appoint the Printer thereof."

44. On 23d March 1731–2, the Report of a Committee on the Derwentwater Estate was read, and it was ordered, "That such a number of Copies of the said Report and Appendix be printed *as shall be sufficient for the use of the Members of the House.*" Derwentwater Estate, 21 Com. Jour. p. 858. A.D. 1731.

45. On

* For the Resolutions by the House of Lords; vide post. paragraphs 64 to 74.

21 Com. Journ. p. 873.

45. And afterwards, on 21st March, it was ordered, *in general terms*, that the same Papers should be printed, by a person appointed by The Speaker.

Charitable Corporation, 21 Com. Jour. p. 897; 1731. Ib. p. 939.

46. On the 20th April it was ordered that such a number of Copies of the Report of the Committee on the Charitable Corporation and Appendix should be printed, as should be *sufficient for the use of the Members*.

47. And on the 1st June they were ordered to be printed, *in general terms*.

York Buildings Company, 21 Com. Journ. p. 149, A.D. 1733.

48. On the 12th May 1733, it was ordered, that such a number of Copies of the Report from the Committee to whom the Petition of the Company for raising the Thames Water in York Buildings is referred, together with the Appendix, be printed as shall be sufficient for the use of the Members of the House.

Ib. p. [illegible].

49. And on the 7th June a motion was made that the Papers relative thereto and the Proceedings of the House thereupon, should be printed (in general terms), upon which the House divided and the motion was negatived.

County Rates Misapplication, Ib. 834. A.D. 1739.

50. On the 3d June 1739, a Report having been presented respecting the misapplication of County Rates, it was ordered, that such a number of Copies of the said Report and Appendix be printed as shall be sufficient for the use of the Members of the House.

Ib. p. 847.

51. On the 10th June, it was ordered, that the said Report, together with the Appendix thereunto, and the Proceedings of the House thereupon, be printed, and that Mr. Speaker do appoint the Printing thereof, and that no person but such as he shall appoint do presume to print the same.

Mode of distribution prior to the recent Order.
Rep. 1822, *Hansard*, p. 198, 200.
Rep. 1828, *Ley*, p. 11, 13.
Bull, p. 19.
Hansard, p. 28.
Rep. 1833, p. 40, Q. 351, 360.
Rep. 1828, *Mitchell*, p. 32, 33.
Nicholls, p. 36.
Rep. 1833, (717.) p. 6, par. 2.
Q. 432 to 436. p. 7, par. 1.
Rep. 1833, (648.) p. 11.
Rep. 1835, (392.) p. xxii and xxx, Res. 14, and Appx. No. 17, p. 110.
Rep. 1835, (606.) p. 9.
And see App. No. 4.

52. From the statements in the Reports referred to in the Margin, and the Evidence subjoined to them, it will appear that a considerable surplus of copies beyond what was required for the use of Members, remained in the stores, under the control of the Officers of the House; and that it was usual for the Speaker to authorize the supply of additional Copies of Papers to such Members as might desire them. The Sale of Parliamentary Papers has always prevailed to a considerable extent, and though not formally authorised, yet with the full knowledge not only of individual Members, but of the Speaker and the Officers of the House.

App. No. 4. p. 87.

53. The Reports and Papers have been deposited in the Library of the British Museum, and other leading Public Libraries, by the authority of the Speaker, for the last 36 years, and likewise a collection of all existing Reports from 1748 to 1800. And by the recommendation of a Committee in 1825 the Reports and Papers are now deposited in the Public Libraries of the Universities of Scotland and Dublin.

Rep. 1825, (516.) p. 4.
Rep. 1831/2, (713.) App. (C.) No. 23, & p. 315.

54. Until a recent period, the supply to the Public appears to have been indefinite, and not subject to any arrangement; the only direct interference being on the part of the Speaker, in regulating the number of Copies to be printed.

The Lords treat the Votes as authorized Publications, 15 Lords' Journ. p. 10, A.D. 1691.
Ib. p. 12.

55. In 1691, upon a Debate concerning the Regulations of the East India Company, on the 30th December, it was resolved that the Printed Vote then read was sufficient ground for that House (the Lords) to take notice of it to the House of Commons; and further, on the 2d January, the Lords prepared certain Heads for a Conference with the House of Commons on the subject: and it is stated that the occasion had arisen "from a Printed Paper, intituled, 'Votes of the House of Commons, Veneris, 18° die Decembris, 1691,' which concludes in these words: 'By virtue of an Order of the House of Commons, I do appoint Thomas Braddyll and Robert Everingham to print these Votes, and that no others do presume to print the same. *J. Trevor*, Speaker.' London, printed by Thomas Braddyll and Robert Everingham, and *are to be sold*

Appendix — (A.) —

sold at the Seaven Starrs in Ave Maria Lane, 1691," and which, as is further stated, contained "matter very proper for their Lordships to take notice of to the House of Commons, as seeming to change the method of proceedings of one House in relation to the other, as likewise that of both Houses to the King.

56. "First,—Because they conceive that the printing and *publishing a resolution* of either House *to address the King* to grant a Charter upon regulations agreed on in one House only, *in order to pass that Charter into an Act of Parliament* is without *precedent*; and,

57. "Secondly,—The printing and publishing a Resolution *of this nature*, of either or both Houses, though in concurrence, may be very *inconvenient*, *because*, addressing to the King for a Charter to make a grant, in the first place under the Great Seal, of things to be passed afterwards into an Act of Parliament, *would invert the method of both Houses* in applying to the King for His Royal Assent, which ought to be done by Bill, and consequently cannot be obtained till after the Bill be passed both Houses; and not by Address, which is to desire the King's consent in the first place, before the Bill be begun in either House."

58. By the Resolution of the 31st December the Lords treat the Printed Votes as a publication sanctioned by this House, and make no complaint of a deviation from ancient usage in the fact of *publication*, but limit the complaint to the *subject-matter*.

59. The proceedings, subsequent on this Vote of the Lords, cannot be traced.

60. On the 21st June 1701, in consequence of the Commons having adopted a Resolution reflecting upon the Lords, in regard to the trial of certain Peers who had been impeached, the Lords complained that "certain Printed Votes of the Commons contained several things highly reflecting upon the House of Peers," and on the 23d declared "that the Resolution of the House of Commons, in their Votes of the 20th June, contained most unjust reflections upon that House, tending to the destruction of the Judicature of the Lords, to the rendering trials on Impeachments impracticable for the future, and to the subversion of the English Government."

Lords' Proceed. vol. 10, pp. 764, 765.

61. The Resolutions of this House had imputed that the Lords "Had refused justice to the Commons, and had proceeded to a pretended trial of Lord Somers, which could tend only to protect him from justice by colour of an illegal acquittal, which proceedings of the Lords being repugnant to justice, were null and void; and farther, that the House of Lords, by the pretended trial, had endeavoured to overturn the right of Impeachment lodged in the Commons by the ancient Constitution, for the safety and protection of the Commons against the power of great men, and had made an invasion on the liberties of the subject, by laying a foundation of impunity for the greatest offences."

62. On the 19th November 1702, the House of Lords was moved to take into consideration the *Votes* of this House, in relation to the Lord Bishop of Worcester, and the appointing a Committee to address the Queen upon the subject.

63. This proceeding had relation to the address (before mentioned) by the Commons, praying the Queen to remove the Bishop from his office of Grand Almoner, on account of alleged interference in an election.

Publication by the House of Lords.

64. On the subject of the discussion concerning the Public Accounts, there are the following entries in the Lords' Journals:

17 Lords' Journ. p. 271. 5 February 1702. 1 Ann.

65. "It is Ordered, by the Lords Spiritual and Temporal in Parliament assembled, that the proceedings of the House, and of the Committee appointed to consider of the observations in the Book of Accompts delivered into this House the 18th of January last, and the 2d day of this instant February, and the Resolution of this House thereupon, shall be forthwith *printed and published*:

66. "It is Ordered, by the Lords Spiritual and Temporal in Parliament assembled, that it shall be and is hereby referred to the same Committee who are appointed to consider of the Observations of the Commissioners of Accompts, to draw up and give directions what shall be *printed and published*.

67. "The

24 Feb. fo. 303.

67. "The House being moved, "That the Report be laid before the Queen, by way of Address,"

68. It was agreed to; and Ordered, that the same Committee do draw up the Address; and the whole proceedings to be *printed and published*."

69. The following is the entry with reference to the Occasional Conformity Act:

Lords' Journals, vol. 17, p. 214; 1702.

70. "The main question was put, 'That the Bill, intituled, An Act for preventing Occasional Conformity, and the amendments made by the Lords to the said Bill, and their reasons for those amendments, and the Commons' reasons, and the Report of the Free Conference thereupon, shall be printed and *published?*"

71. It was Resolved in the affirmative.

Protest against it.

72. "Dissentient, C. Osnaltone, De Longueville.

"Because the printing of Bills and the proceedings on Bills was never done; and therefore is Unparliamentary. It is an appealing to the people, and giving them a pretence of right to examine and judge of the Parliament, which otherwise would be unlawful; and this practice may be of pernicious consequence to the peace of the kingdom, and highly derogatory to the honour and dignity of the House of Lords.

"Sandwich.	"Denbigh.
"Lindsey, G. C.	"Weymouth.
"Nottingham.	"Dartmouth."

Occasional Conformity Bill, &c. to be printed.

73. It is Ordered, by the Lords Spiritual and Temporal in Parliament assembled, that the Bill which was not agreed to, intituled, "An Act for preventing Occasional Conformity," as it came from the House of Commons, and the Bill as amended and agreed to by the Lords, and the Commons' reasons for not agreeing to these amendments, and the reasons of the Lords for insisting on their amendments, and the Report made this day of the Free Conference upon the said Bill, shall be forthwith printed and *published*.

74. Ordered, that the same Committee which drew up what was offered at the Free Conference had in relation to the Bill, intituled, "An Act for preventing Occasional Conformity," do meet to-morrow, at ten o'clock, and give directions accordingly.

Published Resolutions of the House of Lords reflecting upon individuals, 17 Lords' Journ. p. 19.

75. On the 19th January 1701, the Lords ordered the Attorney-General to prosecute William Fuller for the publication of certain books resolved to contain *malicious and scandalous matter*, reflecting upon several Members of both Houses of Parliament, and *dangerous to the Government*, and further ordered that the Votes or Resolutions and Orders made against Fuller and his books should be forthwith printed *and published*.

Ibid. p. 121.

76. On the 16th May 1709, complaint was made to the House (it is presumed by a Peer) of a pamphlet, resolved to be "*a malicious and villanous libel, tending to the subversion of the Monarchy*," and also of a certain Sermon containing expressions giving "*just scandal and offence to all Christians*," and likewise of a certain other pamphlet, resolved to be libellous; and afterwards, on the 21st May, it was reported by a Committee appointed to consider what should be printed upon the Proceedings and Resolutions of the House in relation to some passages contained in the said pamphlets, and thereupon it was ordered that the several Proceedings and Resolutions should be forthwith printed *and published*.

Ibid. p. 143.

16 Lords' Journ. p. 763.

77. In consequence of the Resolutions of the Commons reflecting on the Lords in respect to the trials of the impeached Peers, that House resolved to publish counter resolutions; and on the 23d of June 1701, the Earl of Stamford acquainted the House, "That the Lords' Committee appointed to draw and extract from the books what should be printed in relation to the Lords impeached and the proceedings thereupon, had transcribed a part, but that more remained to be transcribed, whereupon it was ordered what further should be transcribed out of the Journals in order to the printing thereof." And the House of Lords ordered that their several Resolutions passed on that day, with what had been formerly ordered, should be printed, and on the 24th of June the printing is again ordered; whether from the course of proceeding in relation to such printing it was intended for publication this House will judge.

17 Lords' Journ. p. 768.

Appendix —(A.)—

No. 3.

LEGAL DECISIONS AND OBSERVATIONS UPON THE LAW AND PRIVILEGE OF PARLIAMENT.

78. *Thorpe's* case was decided in 1458, at which time the Judges attended in Parliament to advise on matters of Common Law: A question arose upon Privilege, and the Lords entertaining some doubt, called upon the Judges to give their opinion, which they, after deliberation, declined to do, stating, "that they ought not to answer that question, for it hath not been used aforetime that the Justices should *in anywise* determine the Privilege of the High Court of Parliament, for it is so high and so mighty in its nature that it may make law, and that that is law it may make no law; and the determination and knowledge of that Privilege belongeth to the Lords of the Parliament, and not to the Justices." *Thorpe's case, 31 and 32 H. 6. A.D. 1453-4.*

79. This opinion of the Judges was confirmed by that of Lord Coke, who refers to it with approbation, and says, "The Judges ought not to give any opinion of a matter of Parliament, because it is not to be decided by the Common Law, but *secundum legem, et consuetudinem Parliamenti*; and so the Judges in divers Parliaments have confessed." 4th Inst. p. 15.

80. And again, "It doth not belong to the Judges, as hath been said*, to judge of any Law, Custom or Privilege of Parliament." Ib. p. 50.

81. Lord Coke also makes the following note in his Reports: "The *privilege*, order or custom of Parliament, either of the Upper House or of the House of Commons, belongs to the determination or decision *only* of the Court of Parliament." 12 Rep. p. 63.

82. The case of *Joy* v. *Topham* is important, with reference to the present subject. An action was brought against the Serjeant-at-Arms for an assault and false imprisonment in executing a warrant granted by The Speaker against the plaintiff for a breach of the Privilege of the House; the defendant pleaded to the jurisdiction of the Court: which plea was overruled. The Lord Chief Justice Pemberton and Sir T. Jones, two of the Judges who pronounced the decision, were brought to the bar for a breach of the Privilege. The former distinctly affirmed that an Order of the House was pleadable in *bar* to any action for an arrest under it, and also that this House was a superior court of a higher nature than the King's-Bench, and of greater authority, and that the King's-Bench had nothing to do to inspect the actions of this House; and he disclaimed the Court having questioned the legality of the Order or the power, but only whether the party had properly pursued the Order; and Sir T. Jones likewise disclaimed the Court's having questioned the authority of the House, and said, "if the defendant had produced a copy of the Journal, that would have been sufficient, no Judge would have been so silly, or imprudent, at least, to have said that had not been a good and sufficient authority." Both Judges disavowed any intention to decide upon Privilege, and professed to have overruled the plea for *informality*; and Lord Chief Justice Pemberton expressly stated that "for anything *transacted in that House* no other court had any jurisdiction to hear and determine it." *Joy v. Topham, 12 State Trials, p. 821. A.D. 1689.*

83. In *Murray's* case, a Habeas Corpus was applied for to bail a person committed for contempt by the House of Commons and refused, *Wright*, J. observing that it never could have been the intent of the Habeas Corpus Act to give a Judge *or this Court* power to *judge of the Privileges of the House of Commons*. *Murray's case, 1 Wilson, 299. A.D. 1751.*

84. This was followed by *Brass Crosby's* case. He was Lord Mayor of London and a Member of the House of Commons, and was adjudged by the House guilty of a breach of Privilege in having, as Lord Mayor, committed an officer of the House for an alleged assault within the City of London, in executing a warrant against one Miller, who had been voted guilty of a breach of *Crosby's case, 3 Wils. 188. 2 W. Black. 754. 19 State Tri. 1138. A.D. 1771.*

* Lord Coke had just before quoted authorities in proof of his position that the Judges ought not to give an opinion of a matter of Parliament. These words, "as hath been said," manifestly therefore mean, *as he had himself already said*, and not "*as hath been said by some persons*," it being his own express doctrine.

of Privilege. Serjeant Glyn moved to discharge him out of custody, on the ground that the House had exceeded its jurisdiction, by committing for what, on the face of the warrant, did not appear to be a breach of Privilege. De Grey, C. J., in refusing the motion, said, "When the House of Commons *adjudge* any thing to be a contempt or a breach of Privilege, their adjudication is a conviction. This Court cannot take cognizance of a commitment by the House of Commons, because it cannot judge by the same law, for the law by which the Commons judge of their Privileges is unknown to us. The counsel at the bar have not cited one case where any Court of this Hall has determined a matter of Privilege which did not come incidentally before them. Courts of Justice have no cognizance of the acts of the Houses of Parliament, because they belong *ad aliud examen*."*

85. "The House of Commons," says *Gould*, J., "are the only judges of their own Privileges."

86. And Sir *William Blackstone* says, "The privileges and power of the House of Commons are the privileges and power of the *People*. That House is the only Judge of its own proceedings."

87. A similar application by Alderman Oliver to the Court of Exchequer received the same decision.

88. The case of *The Queen* v. *Paty*, excited great interest at the time, having arisen out of the *Aylesbury case* of *Ashby* v. *White*. The defendant had been committed by the House of Commons, and was brought up upon *Habeas Corpus*, when it was solemnly determined that the Court could not enter into the merits of the commitment, and the defendant was remanded. This case is a very strong authority, and the particulars are detailed in a subsequent part of this Report, in relation to the point of incidental jurisdiction. Lord Holt, it is true, differed from the eleven Judges who were consulted on the case, but every Judge from that time has dissented from his opinion.

89. Mr. Justice Blackstone in *Crosby's* case, before referred to, said that Holt differed from the other Judges on the point of the House of Commons being the only Judge of its own privileges, but that the Courts must be governed by the eleven and not by the single one.

90. In *The Queen* v. *Paty*:—Mr. Justice Gould said, "We cannot judge of the Privileges of the House of Commons. The House was entrusted with the liberty of the people, and nobody could suppose they could make any invasions upon it."

91. Mr. Justice Powys—"The House of Commons is a great Court, and all things done by them are to be intended to have been *rite acta*. They are chosen by ourselves, and are our trustees, and it cannot be supposed, nor ought to be presumed, that they will exceed their bounds or do anything amiss. It would be unreasonable to put the Judges upon determining the Privileges of the House of Commons, of which they have no account nor any footsteps in their books."

92. Mr. Justice Powell—"The Commons have a power of Judicature, but not by the Common Law but by the Law of Parliament, to determine their own Privileges. The House of Commons are the supreme Judges of their own Privileges. The Court of Parliament is a superior court to this Court; and though the King's Bench have a power to prevent excesses of jurisdiction in Courts yet they cannot prevent such excesses in Parliament, because that is a superior Court to them."

93. All these and the preceding cases were fully considered in the case of *Burdett* v. *Abbot*; that was an action of trespass brought by Sir Francis Burdett against The Speaker of this House for arresting and imprisoning him.

94. The defendant in his plea relied on the Order of this House as his justification.

95. The Court held that this plea contained a legal justification, after hearing a very learned and elaborate argument on the part of the plaintiff. Lord Ellenborough, in the course of his judgment, says, "Independently of any precedents

precedents or recognised practice on the subject, the House of Commons must *à priori* be armed with a competent authority to enforce the free and independent exercise of its own proper functions." Appendix (A.)

96. This case is very important, as it recognises the principle that Courts of Law have no direct jurisdiction in questions of Privilege.

97. The great learning and ability of the counsel who argued the case on the part of the plaintiff, give assurance that whatever authorities could favour his client were brought forward and the utmost effect given to them. The first point presented to the Court for discussion was, whether it had jurisdiction to entertain the question of Privilege at all, or whether the defendants having shown that they acted under the Orders of the House, did not establish a sufficient defence, upon the ground that the House having resolved that their Privileges had been violated, that Resolution was conclusive upon the question. The counsel did not attempt to contend that the Court had a direct jurisdiction over Privilege; his argument was confined to the position, that where it arose incidentally, the Court had that jurisdiction, and must necessarily exercise it. The answer made by the Attorney-General (Sir Vicary Gibbs) was, that the plaintiff's counsel had cited cases to show "that 14 East, p. 89. where the question of Privilege comes before the Court *incidentally* they must decide it; the plaintiff's argument stopped short, and omitted to show how the question of Privilege arises *incidentally* in this case: on the contrary, if a case were to be invented to show where the question of Privilege arises *directly*, it would be this very case; for here was a direct judgment of the House of Commons, that the plaintiff had been guilty of a breach of their Privileges."

98. The Court determined that the proceedings involved the question of Privilege *directly*, and therefore that the Resolution of the House was conclusive upon the subject.

99. This case was carried by appeal successively to the Exchequer Chamber 4 Taunton, 401, and the House of Lords; and in both tribunals, the judgment of the King's 5 Dow, 165. Bench was affirmed.

100. A Committee of this House was appointed in relation to Sir Francis Burdett's case, which collected many important precedents relating to the Privileges of this House, and of the course of proceeding in respect thereto; and made two Reports, one on the 11th of May 1810, and the other on the 15th of June, to both of which Your Committee beg to refer; and also to the Report See App. (B.) made by a Committee appointed on the 27th of March 1771, "to examine into the several facts and circumstances relative to the then late obstructions to the execution of the orders of the House," in which numerous authorities are collected.

101. The authority most relied upon of a contrary import to those above Benyon v. Evelyn, cited, and to others which might be added, is the case of *Benyon* v. *Evelyn*. Bridgman's Reports, p. 314. That was a decision of Sir Orlando Bridgman, Lord Chief Justice of the A. D. 1664. Court of Common Pleas, in the year 1664.

102. The *dicta* contained in that case are relied upon as impugning the doctrine of the exclusive jurisdiction of Parliament, it would therefore be unfit to pass it by. The plaintiff sued for a debt; the defendant pleaded the Statute of Limitations (that the debt had not accrued within six years); the plaintiff replied that the defendant had had Privilege of Parliament against being impleaded, and therefore could not have been sued within six years.

103. The defendant demurred, and contended that no such privilege existed. By this course of proceeding the Court had no evidence before it respecting the privilege. It was clear that Parliament had passed no Resolution in regard to the particular case: the privilege was claimed, not by the House nor by a Member, but was set up *against a Member*.

104. The Lord Chief Justice says, "I should have been glad not to have Bridgman's Reports, p. 329. had an occasion to have delivered my opinion in this point, for two reasons: First, because it is a tender thing for an inferior court to judge of the Privilege of a superior court; and my Lord Coke (Jurisdiction of Courts, fo. 50) saith, 'The Judges are assistant to the Lords, to inform them of *the common law*;' but it doth not belong to them to judge of any law, custom or privilege *of Parliament*; and cites for it particularly Thorp's case, 31 Hen. 6, Rot. Parl. No. 26, and some other cases; which case only extends where the Privilege of Parliament comes in debate in the House of Peers." He adds, "where

"where upon an action at common law, a question concerning the Privilege of Parliament arises, nothing has been more frequent than for the Judges of the common law to deliver their opinions concerning it, and consequently their judgments. The King himself daily permits his privileges and prerogatives to be determined for him and his subjects in the Courts at Westminster, *by the common law*;*" and proceeds to state, that "in an action when Privilege is part of the plea or justification, it is of necessity that whether there be such Privilege, and the extent of it also, comes into consideration." He there cites 39 Edw. 3, 14, where the judges of assize proceeded in a cause, notwithstanding a resolution and a command to surcease. And several cases are enumerated, most of which are repeated in *Burdett* v. *Abbot*, and commented upon. These cases are directed to show, first, that this House had required the judges of assize to suspend their proceedings against Members in certain causes before them, and which requisitions were upon some occasions not complied with; and also, that Members of Parliament had claimed the privilege of not being impleaded during the Parliament, which privilege had been disallowed by the Judges.

105. Whatever might be the effect of these cases, which it does not seem necessary minutely to examine, the Lord Chief Justice treated them as not having decided the material point, that is, the *jurisdiction of the Court*; because, he says, "that he had been told by the counsel that a Committee of Privileges had declared in favour of the claim during the last Sessions, but that upon inquiry it had been denied;" adding, "so that *it is to me as res integra*;" he proceeds, "but if it be so as was alleged, I shall give all reverence, as becomes me, to all opinions and votes as proceeding from so honourable a body; but I am under the conscience of an oath to do equal law according to the best of my own judgment, whatsoever the authority of other opinions and resolutions may be." It is true the Judge says that he should have judged upon Privilege, notwithstanding a Resolution of the House; but his *decision* goes upon the supposition that *the House had not determined the question*. Considering it was raised by a *creditor against a Member*, in answer to a plea of the Statute of Limitations, Parliament was not directly called upon to interfere. The effect of the decision was, that where the question of Privilege arose *incidentally*, the Court must decide as to its existence and extent, but there is no claim of any jurisdiction to decide upon Privilege *directly*. The effect of this authority of incidental decision will be presently examined.

106. It may not be unimportant to remark, that the Privilege denied by Sir O. Bridgman, is proved to have existed by the fact of its having been modified by three Acts of Parliament, and ultimately rescinded.

107. In estimating the weight of Sir O. Bridgman's judgment, it is proper to observe how he escapes from the authority of *Thorpe's* case, before cited. He avoids the disclaimer of competency in that case, by stating, "the answer of the Judges applies not to the jurisdiction of their own Courts, but to their jurisdiction in Parliament." The insufficiency of this argument is apparent from a fair perusal of the case, wherein the Judges declare that it had not been used for them in *anywise* to determine upon Privilege. The Lords well knew that the Judges had no judicial authority in Parliament, and did not invite them to exercise any, by asking their opinion, nor could the Judges so understand the request. Their reasons for declining to answer were, that the knowledge of Privilege did not belong to them, but to the House: but this was quite as cogent a reason against reviewing the judgment of Parliament upon Privilege in their own Court, as for forbearing to advise when called upon by Parliament so to do. The opinion expressed by Lord Chief Justice Bridgman, which was contrary to that of all the Judges, in *Thorpe's* case, arose from a misapprehension of the meaning they had intended to convey. In *Burdett* v. *Abbot*, the plaintiff's counsel, apparently feeling the pressure of the authority of that case, adopted Sir O. Bridgman's view of it; but that view was entirely repudiated by Lord Ellenborough and Mr. Justice Bayley. When Mr. Holroyd repeated his conception of the meaning of the Judges

* For that reason the courts of common law are the fit tribunals.

Judges when they said, "they were not to *determine* the Privilege of the High Court of Parliament, before which they were then called to advise," Lord Ellenborough said, "the word *determine* was not there meant to be used by them in the sense of *adjudge*, but they meant to say no more than this, 'you, the Lord's House, ask our opinion upon a question before you concerning Privilege of Parliament; but we are not to determine that question; that is, we are not to give you any determinate purpose upon that subject.' The question was not addressed to them as to persons who were to determine or adjudge upon it, but as advisers to the Lords on law. They say, in effect, "*it is not a proper subject for us to enter into; it properly belongs to yourselves, and therefore it is not for us to advise you upon it.*" The judgment in *Thorpe's* case, therefore, was recognised, and the gloss attempted to be put upon it by Sir O. Bridgman disclaimed. Appendix —(A.)—

108. The authorities before mentioned manifest, that Parliament possesses a jurisdiction over matters of Privilege, and that that jurisdiction is exclusive and *final*; but it is urged that although the judgment of Parliament is conclusive upon Courts of Law upon all occasions where the question of Privilege *directly* arises, yet that where it is drawn into question *incidentally* the Court is bound to decide upon it.

109. *Benyon* v. *Evelyn*, before mentioned, is a case in which the Court claimed only the *incidental* jurisdiction, and it is an authority referred to in support of that doctrine. In *The Queen* v. *Paty*, Mr. Justice Powell cites it as an authority to that effect.

110. In *Lord Shaftesbury's* case, Sir T. Jones says, "The cases where the Courts of Westminster have taken cognizance of Privilege differ from this case, for in those *it was only an incident to a case before them which was of their cognizance*, but the *direct* point of the matter now is the judgment of the Lords." And the defendant, who had been committed by the Lords, was remanded. 1 Mod. 144.

111. In the case of *The King* v. *Crosby*, Lord Chief Justice De Grey said, "There is a great difference between matters of Privilege coming *incidentally* before the Court, and being the *point itself* before the Court. In the first case, the Court will take notice of them, because it is necessary to prevent a failure of justice." 3 Wils. 188.

112. In *Burdett* v. *Abbot*, the authority to examine into questions of Privilege arising *directly*, was, after a review of all the previous cases, distinctly repudiated; and the alleged necessity of deciding upon Privileges arising *incidentally*, recognised.

—(D.)—

REPORT FROM THE COMMITTEE

Appointed (upon the 27th day of March 1771) to examine into the several Facts and Circumstances relative to the late Obstructions to the Execution of the Orders of this House; and to consider what further Proceedings may be requisite to enforce a due Obedience thereto; and to report their Proceedings, together with their Opinion, from time to time, to The House.

(The following Title is reprinted in Fac-simile from the Report as originally printed in 1771.)

A

REPORT

FROM THE

COMMITTEE,

APPOINTED

(Upon the 27th Day of MARCH, 1771)

TO EXAMINE INTO

The several FACTS and CIRCUMSTANCES

RELATIVE TO

The late Obstructions to the Execution of the ORDERS of this HOUSE;

AND

To consider what further Proceedings may be requisite to enforce a due Obedience thereto;

And to report their Proceedings, together with their Opinion, from Time to Time, to the House.

Published by Order of the HOUSE *of* COMMONS.

LONDON,

Printed for JOHN WHISTON, at Mr. *Boyle's Head*, and CHARLES BATHURST, at the *Cross Keys*, in *Fleet-street*; LOCKYER DAVIS, opposite *Grays-Inn-Gate*, in *Holbourn*; and WILLIAM BOWYER and JOHN NICHOLS at *Cicero's Head*, in *Red-Lion-Passage, Fleet-street*.

MDCCLXXI.

Appendix —(D.)— Report 1771.

Lunæ, 6 *die Maii*, 1771.

BY *Virtue of an Order of the House of Commons, I do appoint* John Whiston, Charles Bathurst, Lockyer Davis, Benjamin White, *and* William Bowyer *and* John Nichols, *to print this Report*; *and that no other Person do presume to print the same.*

FL[a]. NORTON, Speaker.

Appendix
—(B.)—
Report 1771.

[3]

A

REPORT

FROM THE

COMMITTEE,

APPOINTED

(Upon the 27th Day of MARCH, 1771)

TO EXAMINE INTO

The several FACTS and CIRCUMSTANCES relative to the late Obstructions to the Execution of the Orders of this House;

And to consider what further Proceedings may be requisite to enforce a due Obedience thereto;

And to report their Proceedings, together with their Opinion, from Time to Time, to the House.

THE Committee appointed to examine into the several Facts and Circumstances relative to the late Obstructions to the Execution of the Orders of this House, and to consider what further Proceedings may be requisite to enforce a due Obedience thereto, and to report their Proceedings, together with their Opinion, from Time to Time, to the House, have, in Obedience to the Order of the House, begun by examining into the Facts and Circumstances relating to the late Obstructions to the Orders of the House; and, in order thereto, called before them,

WIlliam Whitham, One of the Messengers attending this House; who said, "That he had had no other Warrant but that "for taking *J. Miller* into Custody, on the Fifteenth of *March* One "Thousand Seven Hundred and Seventy-one: It was directed to

F 2 "Mr.

Appendix
— (B.) —
Report 1771.

[4]

" Mr. *Bonfoy*, Mr. *Clementson*, and himself, with Orders to go and " take *Miller* into Custody; and he proceeded, and came to *Miller's* " House about Two o'Clock; and he asked if *Miller* was at Home, " and was informed he was above Stairs, and would be down in a " little Time; that he waited about a Quarter of an Hour, when " *Miller* came down, and went into his Compting-house; that he " (*Whitham*) followed him, and told him, he hoped he would not be " surprized, that he had the Speaker's Warrant for taking him into " Custody, and offered to shew the Warrant to him; and that he " (*Miller*) just cast his Eye upon it, and said, that the Messenger had " no Authority to take him, and he should take no Notice of it; " whereupon he (the Messenger) laid his Hand upon *Miller's* Arm, " and told him he was his Prisoner, and that he must go with him. " *Miller* said, that he had assaulted him in his own House; and " thereupon told One of the Persons present to go and fetch such " a one, but does not remember the Name of the Constable, who " came in a few Minutes, and *Miller* charged the Constable with " him for the Assault, and required the Constable to carry him be-" fore the Sitting Alderman; that as he (*Whitham*) was going into " the Court where *Miller* lives, he saw a Man, whom he takes to be " the Constable, come out of *Miller's* House, and go into a House " near the Opening into the Court; and, by the Shortness of the " Time, which was about Three or Four Minutes, he judged the " Constable might come from that House; that the Constable came " into the Compting-house, and *Miller* charged him to take the " Messenger (*Whitham*) into Custody; the Constable charged all pre-" sent to assist him, and the Messenger gave the like Charge to all " present on his Behalf; that he is not sure the Constable laid his " Hands on him; but, finding they were determined to arrest him, " he made no Resistance; that he apprehends a Coach was ready by " Order, as there was not Time to call one from the Stand: The " Constable, and one *Clarke*, and *Miller*, and he (the Messenger), " went into the Coach, which was ordered to drive to *Guildhall*, and " did so.

" That, when they arrived at *Guildhall*, they went up Stairs, and " were informed that the Sitting Alderman was gone; that as soon " as they arrived at *Guildhall*, *Clarke* went for Mr. *Clementson*; that " he did not hear any one in particular directed to go to *The Mansion* " *House*; but that several Persons followed *Miller* to *Guildhall*; and " in about a Quarter of an Hour, Word was brought the Sitting " Alderman was at *The Mansion House*; whereupon they went thi-" ther, and were taken into the Room where Business is usually " done: They staid there about a Quarter of an Hour, when Word " was brought that he (*Miller*) could not be examined till Six " o'Clock:—That he (*Whitham*) desired he might not be examined " before Mr. *Clementson* came; that they staid a short Time, when

" a Gentleman

" a Gentleman came and desired *Miller* and him to follow him, who shewed them into a Room where People were dining; they dined, and then went into another Room, where he and *Miller* staid till they were called to the Lord Mayor, who was in his Bed-chamber with Aldermen *Oliver* and *Wilkes*, and several other Persons; that he met Mr. *Clementson* as he was going into the Room to the Lord Mayor. The Lord Mayor began by asking *Miller* concerning his being taken into Custody by the Messenger, and *Miller* gave an Account of it; then the Lord Mayor asked him (the Messenger) By what Authority he took *Miller*? He answered, By the Authority of the Speaker's Warrant, which the Lord Mayor ordered him to produce; he did so, and was ordered by Mr. *Clementson* to read it, but not to deliver it out of his Hands; that as he was going to read it, the Lord Mayor said, he must have the Inspection of it, or no Notice could be taken of it; that he then delivered it to the Lord Mayor, upon his Promise it should be restored to him; that the Lord Mayor took and read it; and he or Mr. *Morris*, but rather thinks the latter, ordered a Copy to be taken of it, and a Copy was taken accordingly:—That the Lord Mayor asked him, if he had applied to any Civil Magistrate to back the Warrant, or whether he was a Peace-Officer? To both which he answered in the Negative:—The Lord Mayor then asked, By what Authority he could take a Citizen into Custody? That he (the Messenger) answered, By the Speaker's Warrant, which he thought sufficient; and the Lord Mayor then said, He had no Authority to take up any one in the City, without his or the Authority of some City Magistrate.

" Then Three Witnesses were sworn to the Facts which passed at *Miller*'s; and that thereupon Mr. *Clementson* informed the Lord Mayor, that he was come by the Speaker's Order to demand the Messenger and his Prisoner: He does not recollect the Answer which was given to this Demand; but some Arguments passed, and Mr. *Morris* spoke a good deal: Then the Lord Mayor said, that he (the Messenger) must be committed to *The Compter*, and *Miller* must be discharged: and ordered a *Mittimus* to be drawn, and that he saw the Lord Mayor sign it: That Mr. *Morris* then said, it would be proper that the other Two Aldermen should sign it, who did so, in the Presence of him the Messenger: The Lord Mayor then said, he did not desire them to be concerned, but would take it upon himself: That, before the Warrant was quite completed, the Lord Mayor or Mr. *Morris* said, there was Bail in the Room, if it was liked of; and one Mr. *Hurford*, Mr. *Withy*, and Mr. *Reynolds* an attorney, offered to be Bail, before the Lord Mayor said, I must give Bail; that he thanked them, but did not know whether he should have Occasion for it; and said that he never had applied to them for it.

Appendix
—(B.)—
Report 1771.

[6]

" That he declined giving Bail, Mr. *Clementson* saying it was not " proper; and the Warrant was signed and sealed: Mr. *Clementson* " then said, that he was ready to give Bail; whereupon the Lord " Mayor grew warm, and said he was trifled with; and that he then " said, that he, or we, would not then take Bail, or Words to that " Purpose; upon which, there was some Noise and Clapping of " Hands in the Room; and there followed some Discourse between " the Lord Mayor, Mr. *Clementson*, and Mr. *Morris*; and he thinks, " in Consequence, it was agreed to take Bail; and *Hurford* and *Withy* " gave Bail, and Mr. *Clementson* agreed to it.

" That Mr. *Clementson* and he (the Messenger) were afterwards " sent back from the Speaker's to *The Mansion House*, for a Copy " of the Warrant of Commitment; and were refused it, being told, " it was not to be found, but, if it should, they might have it in " the morning.—That he (the Messenger) went a Second and Third " Time; and was told the last Time, he might have a Copy of the " Recognizance a little before the Quarter Sessions, if he desired " it; but that the Copy of the Warant was of no Use after Bail " was given."

The Committee then proceeded to examine Mr. *Clementson* the Deputy Serjeant at Arms,—who said, " That he went to the " Speaker's House on *Friday* the Fifteenth of *March*, to see if " the Warrant was signed for taking *Miller* into Custody; that the " Speaker's Secretary had prepared it, and the Speaker signed it, " and delivered it to him (*Clementson*), who gave it to the Messenger, " and told him, that if he found any Difficulty, to send for him, " who should be at Home.—That he heard nothing more, till Half " an Hour past Three o'Clock; then a Person came to him, and " told him, he must come, for that the Messenger was taken up by " a Constable, and charged with an Assault.—That he went to the " Speaker's, and told him of it, who gave him Directions to go and " demand the Messenger, and his Prisoner; and that if Bail was " necessary, he must give it; but that he must see him committed " first.—That he went first to *Guildhall*, about Five o'Clock, but " found nobody there, and was told, he should hear of them at *The* " *Mansion House*.—That he went there, and was introduced to the " Lord Mayor, to his Bed-chamber.—That he told the Lord Mayor, " he understood, that the Messenger, to whom the Warrant was " directed for apprehending *Miller*, was taken up by a Constable, " and charged with an Assault; that he therefore desired to know, " if the Messenger had been brought before him.—That the Lord " Mayor said, he had been told, that a Person, who was called a " Messenger of the House of Commons, had been brought there, " and charged with an Assault.—That he (*Clementson*) waited in an

" Anti-

Appendix —(B.)— Report 1771.

[7]

" Anti-room till Six o'Clock.—That the Messenger then came, and " *Miller* and a Constable (*John Downe*) and a large Concourse of " People.—Then they went in, to the Lord Mayor; Alderman *Wilkes* " and Alderman *Oliver* were there with him.—The Lord Mayor " asked, what was the Purpose of their coming thither? *Miller* said, " he charged *Whitham*, the Messenger, with an Assault. On this, " Mr. *Robert Morris* appeared, and said, he was Counsel for *Miller* " the Prosecutor.—He said, that *Miller* had been violently assaulted, " and falsely imprisoned, by an illegal Warrant.——*Downe*, the " Constable (who was asked for by the Lord Mayor) said, *Miller* " had applied to him, about One or Two o'Clock, and had com- " plained of an Assault on him, in his own House, by the Messenger, " and charged him to take the Messenger into Custody; he there- " fore took him into Custody, in order to carry him before a proper " Magistrate.

" *Miller* was then called upon; who said, That a Person who " called himself a Messenger of the House of Commons came to " him, and took him into Custody, by virtue of a pretended War- " rant.—That *Miller* was then sworn by the Lord Mayor, and said " upon his Oath, that what he had before said was true. He went " on, and said, he had refused to go with the Person.—That the " Person had used Violence, and had seized hold of him, and was " pulling him along.—That the Lord Mayor asked the Messenger, " what Offence *Miller* had committed, or what Authority he had " for assaulting *Miller* in this Manner? The Messenger said, he had " the Speaker's Warrant, directed to him, to take *Miller* into Custody. " The Lord Mayor asked where the Warrant was? That he (*Cle- " mentson*) told *Whitham* to open it, and read it himself.—That the " Lord Mayor or Mr. *Morris* (he can't say which) said it must be " produced.—That he (*Clementson*) objected to it for some Time; " but the Lord Mayor saying it could not be taken Notice of, if " not produced, he delivered it to the Lord Mayor, on his pro- " mising to deliver it back to him; that he waited till this Time, to " see the Nature of the Assault charged on *Whitham*; and finding " that it was for executing the Warrant for taking *Miller* into " Custody, he then told the Lord Mayor, that he appeared before " him as Deputy Serjeant at Arms of the House of Commons; that " he came there by the Speaker's Directions, and had his Commands " to demand not only *Whitham* the Messenger, but likewise *Miller* " his Prisoner; and he made that Demand in the most solemn " Manner he was able.—That Mr. *Morris*, on this, desired he (*Cle- " mentson*) might be sworn as an Evidence:—But he (*Clementson*) de- " clared he would not be sworn, and said, he did not come as an " Evidence, but as an Officer of the House of Commons, to exe- " cute the Commands given him by the Speaker.—The Lord Mayor " said, he could not take Notice of any Thing in his Magisterial

F 4 " Capacity,

Appendix
—(B.)—
Report 1771.

[8]

"Capacity, that was not given upon Oath.—That he was then asked by *Morris*, if he refused to be examined to any of the Facts or Circumstances within his Knowledge.—That he doubted at first what Answer to give to that; but, on Recollection, he said, if there was the least Doubt either of the Warrant being signed by the Speaker, or of his (*Clementson*'s) having the Speaker's Commands to demand *Whitham* the Messenger and *Miller* his Prisoner, he was ready to be sworn to the Truth of those Matters; but would not be sworn generally.—Finding that to be his Resolution, Mr. *Morris* declined swearing him as to those Matters; but he (*Clementson*) again repeated, that if there was any Doubt as to those Matters, he was ready to swear to them.

"That the Lord Mayor asked *Whitham* if he was a Peace Officer or a Constable? he said, he was not;—if he had applied to any City Magistrate to back his Warrant? he said he had not:—Upon this, the Lord Mayor declared, That it was very extraordinary for any Citizen to be taken up in the City of *London*, without the Knowledge or Authority of the Lord Mayor, or some other Magistrate of the City; and if this was permitted to be the Case, it would be trampling on the Laws, and there would be an End of the Constitution of this Country.

"Then *Miller* was examined, as to his being a Livery-man of the City of *London*.—The Lord Mayor said, it was his Opinion, that no Warrant, but from him or some other Magistrate of the City, was good and valid to take up any Citizen; that he thought himself bound, so long as he held the great Office of Chief Magistrate of the City of *London*, to take Notice of a Proceeding of this Sort; and that it was his Duty to defend the Citizens, and their Rights and Liberties, to the last Extremity.—He said, he was of Opinion, the Messenger had no Right to take up *Miller*, who was a Citizen, not being charged with any Felony, Trespass, or Breach of the Peace.

"That Mr. *Morris* then took Four Objections to the Warrant:

"First, that the Words ["House of Commons"] was not a sufficient Description of the Power which had passed the Vote.—That it should have been, ["The House of Commons in Parliament assembled."]

"Secondly, That ["*J. Miller*"] was no sufficient Description of the Person.

"Thirdly, That the Offence was not inserted; and therefore that it was illegal, and without Colour of Law.

"Fourthly, That it did not appear, that ["*Fletcher Norton*, Speaker,"] who signed the Warrant, was the Sir *Fletcher Norton*, who is Speaker of the House of Commons.

"That the Lord Mayor asked *Whitham*, whether he intended to carry *Miller* away as his Prisoner? *Whitham* said, he did.—The

"Lord

[9]

" Lord Mayor then said, he thought the Warrant was illegal; and therefore he discharged *Miller* out of the Custody of the Messenger; and said at the same Time, This Citizen comes here to claim a Citizen's Protection of me, and I think he is entitled to it.

" That then the Lord Mayor proceeded on the Assault.—*Miller* proved that *Whitham* had laid hold of his Arm and pulled him; and that about Five Minutes afterwards, the Constable came. After this, Three Persons were produced to prove the Assault:

" *Henry Page*, of *Newgate-street*, Printer.
" *John Topping*, of *The Old Bailey*, Printer.
" *Robert Page*, of *Newgate-street*, Printer.

" They proved, that *Whitham* laid hold of *Miller*'s Arm, and said, he was his Prisoner; and that *Miller* said, he should not go, or did not chuse to go. That *Whitham* said, You must go; and *Miller* said, he should not; and then *Whitham* charged every body present to assist him. After this, the Constable was brought; and the Constable charged all present to assist him.

" That the Lord Mayor, on this, gave it as his Opinion, that the Assault was fully proved; and that *Whitham* must give Security to appear at the next Session for the City of *London*, to answer such Indictments as should be then found against him for the Assault and false Imprisonment, himself in Forty Pounds, and Two Securities in Twenty Pounds each; and that *Miller* was to be bound to appear and make out the Charge.—Mr. *Morris*, and many others present, were ready to be Bail for *Whitham*: That *Whitham* was very much frightened, and was ready to offer Bail; but he (*Clementson*) insisted he should not give Bail.—The Lord Mayor desired it might be noticed, that Bail was offered; but not accepted by *Whitham*.

" Then the Lord Mayor directed a Warrant to be made out; and the Person who had these Directions he saw fill up what he supposed was the Warrant; and the Lord Mayor declared, it was a Warrant for committing *Whitham* to *The Compter*.—That he saw the Lord Mayor sign that Paper.—On this, Mr. *Morris* desired the other two Aldermen might sign the Warrant, as well as his Lordship; else it might be supposed, that they did not concur in Opinion with his Lordship.—The Lord Mayor said, he did not desire any body else to sign it, though the Two Aldermen declared themselves ready to do it; and he particularly said to Alderman *Wilkes*, *I think you have enough upon your Hands already*.—The warrant however was directed to be altered by the Clerk into the Plural Number; and he saw that Paper signed by the other Two Aldermen, *Wilkes* and *Oliver*.—That he asked the Lord Mayor, if it was signed by them all; and he said, it was; and Directions were given by the Lord Mayor and Mr. *Wilkes* to the Constable, that he (*Whitham*) might be used kindly in Prison.—That just before they were

G "going

Appendix
— (B.) —
Report 1771.

[10]

"going to take him away, he thought that, this being a Commitment, he had gone far enough; and then he offered Bail.—That the Lord Mayor grew warm at this, and said, that he found that this Proceeding meant to exaggerate the Offence, or Business, or the Proceeding; he could not recollect exactly the Word he made Use of.

"That, after this was done, he came back immediately to the Speaker; and upon his relating what had happened, he desired him to go back and try to get a Copy of the Warrant of Commitment.—The Lord Mayor said, he could not tell where to find it then, every body being gone away; but that if it was not destroyed, being now of no Use, he should have a Copy; but that I knew he had signed it alone first, and that afterwards Alderman *Wilkes* and Alderman *Oliver* desired to sign it too; and that he and Alderman *Oliver* should, in their Places in the House of Commons, admit their having signed such a Warrant; but that he should have a Copy of it in the Morning if it could be found.—That he applied again on *Saturday* Morning to the Lord Mayor for a Copy of the Warrant; he said he could not yet find it; that some of them had taken it away, and he knew not where it was, but that if it could be found, *Whitham* should have a copy of it; that it did not signify, for that he did not mean to deny what had been done, or make Use of any Subterfuge; and that this was all that he (*Clementson*) had done.——That he did not go to execute the Warrant himself; and that it was not sealed.

"And he further added this Circumstance, that he recollects, when the Lord Mayor had signed the *Mittimus*, and he the Deputy Serjeant had offered Bail, the Lord Mayor grew warm, and made Use of some Expression, that he should not take Bail then, or Words to that Purpose; saying, that this Proceeding meant to exaggerate the Offence, or Words to that Effect; but he soon afterwards said, he must take Bail.

"That he endeavoured to serve the Order of the House on *J. Wheble*; and went on *Thursday* the 28th *February*, to his (*Wheble's*) Shop, and enquired for him, and the Servant said, he was not at Home, but would be in an Hour's Time; that he called again, and received the same Answer;—that he called again, and was answered by a Lad in the Shop, who said he was an Apprentice, that he was not at Home, being gone to the other End of the Town; and that his Master had waited all the Day before, expecting him.—That he (*Clementson*) then said, that he would call again in an Hour, and bid him tell his Master.——That he did so; and was told, he (*Wheble*) had been in, and was gone out again; but if he would let him know where he (*Clementson*) might be found, he would wait on him.—That he went to a Coffee-house, and waited;

"then

Appendix
— (B.) —
Report 1771.

[11]

" then called again, and was told, *Wheble* was expected to Dinner at Three o'Clock ——That he called at Half an Hour past Three, and was told *Wheble* was not at Home, but would be soon.—That he called again at Four and Five o'Clock, and received the same Answers.——That he left Word, he was the Deputy Serjeant at Arms, and would be there again at Half an Hour past Nine in the Morning; which he accordingly was, and was told by the same Person, that *Wheble* was not at Home, but said, he had delivered the Message he had left with him, and that his Master said, he was very sorry he was obliged to go out, and he left no Word when he would be at Home.—That he called again at Eleven o'Clock, and he was not at Home; but was answered, he might be in, in Half an Hour.—That he went again on *Saturday* at Ten o'Clock, and the Apprentice said, he was not at Home, but would be in the Afternoon; and said it with a Smile, as if laughing at my frequent calling; and said, if he would leave Word where he might be found, we will send you Word when he is at Leisure.—That he (*Clementson*) said, he would be there at Seven o'Clock, which he accordingly was, but was told, he (*Wheble*) was not at Home, and had sent for his Linen, and therefore was not expected till *Monday*.

" That he did not go to *Thompson* till *Friday* the First of *March*, because there were Two *R. Thompsons*, one *Richard*, the other *Robert*.—That he found, at the Stamp-Office, that *Thompson* had been summoned before the Commissioners to give Security and said his Name was *Robert* :—That he sent a Messenger to enquire in the Neighbourhood, and found there was but One :—That he went to *Thompson's* House, and was told by a Man he was not at Home, nor could tell when he would be, or whether he was in Town; that he had seen him Two or Three Days before; that nobody knew more about *Thompson* than himself, and if he (*Clementson*) would leave a Message, he would deliver it :—That *Williams* the Messenger then said, You know our Business; to which he made no Answer :—That he went again at Eleven o'Clock; and the Servant said, *Thompson* was not at home; for he had not seen him, and nobody knew better than he; and said, that if he (*Clementson*) had Business with *Thompson*, it was usually left with him first, and that no time was more likely to meet with him than that Day or To-morrow.

" That he (*Clementson*) went again on *Saturday*; and the same Person told him *Thompson* was not at Home, but would be in Half an Hour, but had no Reason for thinking so: That he went Twice afterwards, and he was not at Home, nor had been, and that he did not know when he would be :—That he (*Clementson*)

Appendix
—(B.)—
Report 1771.

[12]

" said, Then he will not see me; and received for Answer, he could " not tell."

And he further said, "That there had been One more Attempt " since, to execute the Warrants on *Wheble* and *Thompson*; that Mr. " *Speaker* had made an Alteration in the Direction of the Warrants, " by inserting the Name of *Wood* the Messenger; that *Wood* took " the Warrant, and he (*Clementson*) followed after, to endeavour to " find *Wheble* and *Thompson*; that he (*Clementson*) waited at a Coffee-" house in *Wheble*'s Neighbourhood; that *Wood* went and endea-" voured to find them, but without Effect."

Your Committee then proceeded to examine *Charles Williams* the Messenger; who said, "he attended the Serjeant, in endeavouring " to serve the Warrants on *Wheble* and *Thompson*, on *Thursday* the " Twenty-eighth Day of *February*:—That he went Six or Seven " Times to *Wheble*'s House; that he did not find him at Home, but " was told he would be at Home soon.

" That he went to *Thompson*'s several Times, and received the " same sort of Answers; that the Business they came upon was " known at both Places; and that he had read Mr. *Clementson*'s " Minutes at the Time, which he found were right."

The Committee then proceeded to examine *Guy Wood* the Messenger; who said, "He had the Speaker's Warrant, about the " Tenth or Eleventh of *March*, to arrest *Thompson* and *Wheble*; that " he received it from the Deputy Serjeant; that his (*Wood*'s) Name " was inserted in the Warrant; that he went with one Mr. *Lee* to " *Thompson*'s House; that *Lee* went in, and enquired for *Thompson*; " that they had agreed, that, if *Lee* staid above a Minute, he " (*Wood*) was to come in after him; but *Lee*, not finding him at " Home, came out immediately.

" That they went from thence to *Wheble*'s, and proceeded in the " same Manner. *Lee* went in, and was told *Wheble* was gone into " the Country: They then went to the *Green Dragon* in *Fleet-street*, " where *Wheble*'s Evening Papers are delivered, and staid some time, " to try if they could see him come after his Papers, or about his " Business, but could see nothing of him: That they have made " several Enquiries since, and can hear nothing of him."

Your Committee having thus stated the Evidence of the Facts and Circumstances relative to the late Obstructions to the Execution of the Orders of this House, as it appeared before them, proceeded to the other Part of what was given them in Charge; namely, "To " consider

[13]

" consider what further Proceedings may be requisite to enforce a " due Obedience to the Orders of the House;" and, in order to form their Judgement upon that Matter, they have made a diligent Search in the Journals, to see what the Proceedings of the House have been on similar Occasions; or, if no Cases strictly analogous should occur, at least to deduce, from the general Practice of the House, such Principles of Parliamentary Law as might be applicable to the present Matter referred to their Consideration.

And in this Place the Committee beg Leave to observe, that it appears to them that this House has, from the earliest Times, asserted and exercised the Power and Authority of summoning before them any Commoner, and of compelling his Attendance;——and that this Power and Authority has ever extended as well to the City of *London*, without Exception on account of Charters from the Crown, or any Pretence of separate Jurisdiction (Instances of which appear in the Cases referred to in the Margin), as to every other Part of the Realm.

Ferrers' Case, in Crompton, Fo. 9 & 10.—Seymour, 6 E. VI. 1st vol. p. 25.—Bassett, 1 & 2 P. and M. 1555.—Nov. 30, 1st vol. p. 44.—Courtenay, 5 & 6 P. and M. 1557, Nov. 10, 1st vol. p. 61.—Sir Servants of Sir H. Jones, 20 Feb. 1568, 1st vol. p. 83.—Wm. Jones, 29 Oct. 8 Eliz. 1566, 1st vol. p. 75.—Sir J. Shirley, March 29, 1603, 1st vol. p. 169.—Searing, 1664, vol. viii. p. 538.—5 Jan. 1673, vol. ix. p. 284. "That it is against the King's Dignity nor the House of Commons to punish, by Imprisonment, a Commoner that is guilty of violating their Privileges, that being according to the known Laws and Customs of Parliament, and the Right of their Privileges, declared by the King's Royal Predecessors in former Parliaments, and by himself in this."—1 April 1707, vol. xi. p. 155, John Salisbury.—3 Jan. 1705, vol. xiv. p. 839, Tutchin, How, and Bragg.—27 May 1721, vol. xix. p. 564, Blue.

And that the House have ever considered every Branch of the Civil Authority of this Government as bound (when required) to be aiding and assisting to carry into Execution the Warrants and Orders of this House.

In

Appendix
—(B.)—
Report 1771.

[14]

In order to lay before the House the Result of their Enquiry with tolerable Brevity, and some Degree of Method, the Committee have reduced under Three General Heads the Obstructions which have been given at different Times to the Orders of the House, and under each of these Heads have ranged the different Modes in which these Breaches of Privileges and Contempts have been offered; and then submit to the Consideration of the House the several Methods of Proceeding which the House hath opposed to these Offences, the Proofs of which Proceedings appear by Cases referred to in the Margin of this Report.

The Three General Heads of Breaches of Privilege and Contempts of this House are, namely, those arising from,

First, Evasion.
Secondly, Force.
Thirdly, Colour of Law.

Offences under the First and Second of these Heads have been committed—by the absconding of the Parties summoned—by open Resistance to the Officers of the House—and by Riots and Tumults—by the Refusal of Civil Officers to assist the Serjeants or Messengers of this House, or to release Persons entitled to the Privilege of this House when detained in their Custody.

It appears also to your Committee, as well from searching the Journals of this House as from other authentic Evidence, that, in order to remedy the Abuses and to remove the Obstructions above recited, this House has proceeded to support their Privileges, and to enforce the Execution of their Orders, by the following Methods; namely,

I. By addressing the Crown to issue Proclamations for apprehending those Persons who thus stand in Contempt of the House (1).

(1) Sir Giles Mompesson, [illegible] Feb. and 3 March 1620, vol. i. p. [illegible].—Windebank, Dec. 10, 1640, vol. ii. p. [illegible].—Sir Basil Brook, April [illegible], 1641, vol. ii. p. [illegible].—Sir John Lloyd, &c. Jan. 9, 1680, vol. ix. p. [illegible].—Brent, Feb. [illegible], 1680, vol. x. p. [illegible].—Sir Adam Blair, June 14, 1689, vol. x. p. [illegible].—Standish, March [illegible], 1694, vol. xi. p. [illegible].—Mackenzie, vol. ix. p. [illegible].—[illegible], Nov. [illegible], 1696, vol. xi. p. [illegible].—[illegible], April 22, 1702, vol. xiii. p. [illegible].—Jeffreys,

II.

Appendix
—(B.)—
Report 1771.

[15]

—Jeffreys, Addy, and Chi[illegible], March 16 and 20, 1701, vol. xiii. p. [illegible], 430, 437.—Colepeper and others, March 20, April 6, 1702, vol. xiv. p. [illegible].—Tutchin, &c. Printers, Feb. 10, 1703, vol. xiv. p. 336.—[illegible], in [illegible] Case, March 24, 1709, and 6th, 1709, vol. xvi. p. 343, 346.—[illegible], 1 and 2 Feb. 1715, vol. xviii. p. [illegible].—Williamson, 9 June and 5 July 1721, vol. xix. p. [illegible].—Loveland, 4 March 1740, vol. xxv. p. 613.—A. Murray, 26 Nov. 1751, vol. xxvi. p. [illegible].—Raymond, 11, 14, 15, 16, and 18th Feb. 1768, vol. xxxi. p. [illegible], [illegible], 610, 616, 620.

(2) Harvey and Morris, [illegible] April 1713, 17th vol. p. [illegible].—Ingoldsby, 29 Jan. 1714, 20th vol. p. 340.—Pickles and Brown, 29 Jan. 1733, 22d vol. p. 210.—A. Murray, as above.

II. By renewing their Orders against such Persons and committing them in a subsequent Session of Parliament (2).

(3) Bagshaw, 14 Nov. 1640, vol. ii. p. [illegible].—Sir Basil Brook, Jan. 11 and 25, 1641, vol. ii. p. 372.—Nokes and Thompson, 21 Dec. 1660, vol. viii. p. 222.—Dudley, 24 Jan. 1670, vol. ix. p. [illegible].—Topham, 4 June 1678, P. M. vol. ix. p. 486.

III. By Orders to Mayors, Bailiffs, and Sheriffs, to assist the Serjeant or Messenger for the apprehending of such Persons; or to the Serjeant of this House, to call on the Sheriffs of *Middlesex*, and the Sheriffs of other Counties, and all other Magistrates and Persons, for their Assistance (3).

(4) Hastings and Crook, 19 May 1674, vol. ix. p. 341.—Topham, as above.—Blythe, 7 April 1679, vol. ix. p. 587.—Owen, 26 March 1702, vol. xiii. p. 826.

IV. By committing, for Breach of Privilege of this House, those Officers of the Peace who have refused their Assistance to the Serjeant of this House when so called on (4).

(5) Ferrers.—Sir T. Shirley and Sterling, as above.

V. By imprisoning those who refused to release Persons entitled to the Privilege of this House, and by increasing the Severity of their Restraint, according to the Nature of the Offence, and in Consequence of the Contumacy of the Offender (5).

G 4 With

Appendix
—(B.)—
Report 1771.

[16]

With regard to the Third Head—namely, Breaches of Privilege, and Contempts of this House, under Colour and Pretence of Law; It appears to your Committee that the same have been attempted, by discharging out of Custody Persons who had been committed by Order of the House:

By impleading, in the Courts of Justice, Persons entitled to the Privilege of this House, in the Cases there brought in Question.

By Prosecutions, before the said Courts, for Words or Actions spoken or done under the Protection of this House.

By Accusations, tending to call in Question before the said Courts Words or Actions so spoken or done, under false or pretended Denominations of Offences, not entitled to the Privilege of this House.

It appears also to your Committee, in searching the Journals, that in the above recited Instances this House has proceeded,

1st, By taking again into Custody Persons discharged without Order of the House (6).

(6) Pemberton and others, 8 June 1675, vol. ix. p. 351.—Duncomb, March 22, 1697, vol. xii. p. 176; when the House Resolved, That no Person committed by this House can, during the same Session, be discharged by any other Authority whatsoever. Charles Duncombe having been committed by Order of this House, and afterwards discharged by the Order of the House of Lords, without the Consent of this House; it was Resolved, That the said Charles Duncombe be taken into the Custody of the Serjeant at Arms attending this House.

2dly, By directing Mr. Speaker to write Letters to the Justices of Assize, and other Judges, to stay proceedings (7).

(7) Strickland, 19 March [illegible], vol. i. p. [illegible].—Pene, 8 Feb. [illegible], vol. i. p. 521.—[illegible], 23 and 27 Feb. [illegible], for Stay of Trial, as to other like Cases has been moved, vol. i. p. 841, 842. Sir R. Chargrave,

3dly,

Appendix
—(B.)—
Report 1771.

[17]

gave, Sir W. Kingswell, [illegible].—Bond, Feb. 28, 1606, vol. i. p. 341.—Hyatt, 3 March 1606, vol. i. p. 346.—Pewbest, 5 May 1607, vol. i. p. 369.—Bullingham, 13 May 1607, vol. i. p. 373.—[illegible], 20 May 1607, vol. i. p. 376.—Johnson, 10 June 1607, vol. i. p. 381.—Brown, 20 June 1607, vol. i. p. 386.—Pelham, 8 May 1610, vol. i. p. 422.—Sandys, 18 and 21 May 1610, vol. i. p. 429.—"General Motion about Letters to be written to the Justices of Assize, referred to the Committee of Privileges, report this Resolution: Resolved, that the former Course of writing Letters to the Justices of Assize, according to Precedents; and, if required, a Warrant for Inhibition to the Party," 3 March 1620, vol. i. p. 537.—Lord Bulkley, 28 April 1691, vol. x. p. 537.

(8) Sir Robert Howard 17 Feb. 1625, vol. i. p. 820.—Sir Wm. Williams, 7 Feb. 1685, vol. x. p. 91, 149, and 215.—Bolle and others, 6 July 1641, vol. ii. p. 201 and 202.—Jay and Topham, 4 June 1689, vol. x. p. 64, 210, 212, & 227.—Edward, 13 and 14 April 1716, vol. xviii. p. 430; and on the 18 April the Clerk of the Peace was ordered to attend the House at the Table.

3dly, By Resolutions of this House, That the Suits and Actions commenced and carried on in these Cases should be discontinued and annulled, and should be deemed Violations of the Privileges of this House (8).

(9) Case of the Five Members, 23 Jan. 1641, vol. ii. p. 387.—Jay and Topham, as above.

4thly, By committing those Judges who have proceeded to the Trial of, or pronounced Sentence upon, Persons entitled to the Privilege of this House, for Words or Actions spoken or done under the Protection of the Privilege of this House (9).

n Your

Appendix
— (B.) —
Report 1771.

[18]

Your Committee have selected a few Cases, from among the many referred to in the Margin of this Report, which, from the Nature of their Circumstances, or the Importance of the Doctrine which they illustrate, or the Consequences which they produced, seemed to your Committee fit to be more fully stated than the Margin would admit; and are therefore added as an Appendix to this Report.

Your Committee beg Leave to observe, that in the diligent Search they have made in the Journals, they have not been able to find an Instance, that any Court or Magistrate has presumed to commit, during the Sitting of Parliament, an Officer of the House, for executing the Orders of the House.

They farther beg Leave to observe, that they have not been able to find, that there has ever been an Instance, wherein this House has suffered any Person, committed by Order of this House, to be discharged, during the same Session, by any other Authority whatsoever, without again committing such Person.

And therefore, with regard to *J. Miller*, who was delivered from the Custody of the Messenger by the Lord Mayor, who for the said Offence is now under the Censure of the House; as it appears to your Committee, that it highly concerns the Dignity and Power of the House, to maintain its Authority in this Instance, by re-taking the said *J. Miller*—The Committee recommend to the Consideration of the House,

Whether it may not be expedient, that the House should order That the said *J. Miller* be taken into the Custody of the Serjeant at Arms attending this House.

And that the Serjeant at Arms, his Deputy or Deputies, be strictly enjoined to call upon the Magistrates, Officers of the Peace, and other Persons, who, by the Terms of the Speaker's Warrant, are required to be aiding and assisting to him in the Execution thereof, for such Assistance as the said Serjeant, his Deputy or Deputies, shall find necessary to enable him or them to take into Custody the said *J. Miller*.

APPENDIX.

APPENDIX.

CROMPTON on Jurisdiction of Courts, Fo. 9, 10.

"IN the 34th of *Henry* the VIIIth, one *George Ferrers*, a Burgess for the Town of *Plymouth*, was arrested in *London*, by a Process out of the King's Bench, at the Suit of one *White*; of which the House being informed, ordered the Serjeant to repair to *The Compter* in *Bread-street*, whither the said *Ferrers* was carried, and there to demand the Delivery of the Prisoner. The Serjeant went to *The Compter*, and declared to the Clerks there, what he had in Commandment; but the Clerks and other Officers of the City, after many high Words, forcibly resisted the Serjeant. Whereupon ensued a Fray, in which the Serjeant's Man was knocked down, and the Serjeant was driven to defend himself with his Mace of Arms. During this Fray, the Sheriffs of *London*, called *Rowland Hill* and *H. Suckley*, came thither, to whom the Serjeant complained of this Injury, and required of them the Delivery of the Prisoner; but they took Part with their Officers, and gave no Attention to his Complaint, and contemptuously refused to deliver the Prisoner. The Serjeant returned to the House, and made his Report of the above Transaction; who thereupon would sit no longer without their Burgess; but rose and repaired to the Upper House, where the whole Case was declared by the Mouth of the Speaker, before the Lord Chancellor and all the Lords and Judges there assembled, who, judging the Contempt to be very great, referred the Punishment thereof to the Order of the House of Commons; who, being returned to their House, ordered the Serjeant to repair immediately to the Sheriffs of *London*, and to require the Delivery of the Prisoner, without any Writ or Warrant, though the Lord Chancellor offered to grant a Writ, which the House of Commons refused, being clearly of Opinion, that all Commands, and other Acts proceeding from their House, were to be done and executed by their Serjeant, without Writ, only by Shew of his Mace, which was his Warrant.——The Sheriffs, upon this Second Demand, delivered the Prisoner; but the Ser-

 "jeant,

Appendix
—(B.)—

Report 1771.

[20]

" jeant, in Pursuance of his Orders, charged the said Sheriffs to " appear before the House the following Day, by Eight of the " Clock in the Morning, and to bring thither the Clerks of *The Comp-* " *ter*, and such other of their Officers as were Parties to the Fray.— " The Serjeant had also Orders to take into Custody the said *White*, " who had procured the said Arrest, in Contempt of the Privilege " of Parliament. The Sheriffs, on the next Day, with One of the " Clerks of *The Compter* who was the chief Occasion of the Fray, " together with the said *White*, appeared before the House; where " the Speaker charging them with their Contempt and Misdemeanor " aforesaid, they were compelled to make immediate Answer, with- " out being admitted to any Counsel, although Sir *Robert Cholmley*, " then Recorder of *London*, and other the Counsel of the City there " present, offered to speak in the Cause, which were all put to Silence, " and none suffered to speak but the Parties themselves. Whereupon, " in Conclusion, the said Sheriffs and *White* were committed to *The* " *Tower of London*; and the said Clerk, who was the Occasion of " the Fray, to a Place there called *Little Ease*, and the Officers of " *London* called *Taylor*, with Four other Officers, who had arrested " *Ferrers*, were committed to *Newgate*.

" The King, being informed of this Proceeding, called before " Him the Lord Chancellor of *England*, and the Judges, with the " Speaker, and many others of the House of Commons, to whom He " declared His Opinion to this Effect: He commended their Wisdom " in maintaining the Privileges of their House; He, among other " Things, further declared, That he was informed by His Judges, " that He at no Time stood so highly in His Estate Royal, as in " the Time of Parliament, when He as Head, and they as Members, " are conjoined and knit together, into One Body Politic; so as " whatsoever Offence or Injury during that Time is offered to the " meanest Member of the House, is to be judged as done against " His Royal Person, and the whole Court of Parliament; which " Prerogative of the Court is so great (as his Learned Counsel in- " form Him) that all Acts and Processes coming out of any other " Inferior Courts, must for the Time cease, and give Place to the " Highest.

" Whereupon Sir *Edward Montagu*, then Lord Chief Justice, " declared his Opinion, confirming by divers Reasons what the " King had said; which was assented to by all the rest, none speaking " to the contrary."

This Case is also referred to by Sir *Robert Atkyns*, in his Tract on the Power, Jurisdiction, and Privilege of Parliament, and in *Dyer's* Reports.

Sir

[21]

Sir Robert Howard's CASE, 17 *February*, 1625.

Vol. I. p. 820.

" Motion made, where Sir *Robert Howard*, during Privilege of " Parliament, was excommunicated for not taking the Oath *ex Officio*.

" Resolved, upon Question, To refer this to the Examination of " a Select Committee, Mr. *Selden* and others.

" This Committee to take Consideration of the Restraint and " Excommunication of Sir *Robert Howard*; and to make their Re- " port to the House of their Proceedings and Opinions therein," p. 821.

March 21, p. 839. " Mr. *Selden* reports from the Committee, " That Sir *Robert* stood privileged by the House, when these Pro- " ceedings were had against him.—That, upon his Appearance be- " fore the Court, an Oath was tendered him, to answer Things " objected against him; he answered, he was a Burgess of Parlia- " ment. They pressing him notwithstanding to answer, they at length " committed him close Prisoner to *The Fleet*. Having laid Two Days, " he petitioned the Lord Keeper for a *Corpus cum Causa*; and upon " Mr. *Bembow's* Certificate, that he was a Parliament Man, the Lord " Keeper enlarged him by the 10th of *March*.—That Day the " Court of High Commission pressed him again to answer; he " claimed the Privilege of Parliament again; they (the Parliament " approaching) gave him Time of Deliberation. On the 15th of " *March* the Parliament sat and adjourned. On the 17th of *March* " they called him again; when he brought them the Copy of the " Indenture of Return under *Bembow's* Hand, and the Copy of the " *Habeas Corpus* upon which he had been delivered. That he " being again pressed to answer, and he claiming Privilege as before, " they, because he shewed no Record to prove him a Parliament " Man, pronounced him *Contumax*, and excommunicated him; or- " dering him further, he should, before the 19th of *March*, attend " One of the Commissioners, and be bound in Three Thousand Pounds " to appear the *Wednesday* after, and stand to the Order of the " Court.

" Resolved, upon Question, That Sir *Robert Howard* ought to " have had Privilege of Parliament, *Nem. Con.*

" Secondly, Resolved, upon Question, That Sir *Robert Howard* " claimed his Privilege of Parliament in due Manner, *Nem. Con.*

 " Resolved,

[22]

" Resolved, upon Question, That a Day be assigned to the " Members of our House, and those others which are Contemners, " to answer in the House their Proceedings against Sir *Robert* " *Howard*.—This to be done upon *Friday* next, Nine o'Clock.

" Those of our own Members to be made acquainted with the " Day; for the other Contemners, a Warrant shall issue under Mr. " *Speaker* his Hand, for their Appearance that Day."

3d *May*, p. 854. " Sir *John Hayward* called in about Sir *Robert* " *Howard*'s Business, and interrogated by Mr. *Speaker*, &c.

" Dr. *Pope* called in, and interrogated.

" Mr. *Mottersey*, the Register, called in, and interrogated.

" Upon Question, All the Proceedings in the High Commission " Court against Sir *Robert Howard*, from the 1st of *February*, 22 " *James*, at which Time he ought to have had his Privilege of " Parliament, declared to be void, and ought to be vacated and " annihilated.

" Secondly, Upon Question, Whether a Letter to be written, by " Mr. *Speaker*, to the Lord of *Canterbury* and the rest of the Lords " and others of the High Commissioners, for annulling of the said " Proceedings. The House divided. Carried for the Negative.

" Upon Question, Sir *John Hayward*, Dr. *Pope*, and the Register, " called in; and the Effect of the said Order declared to them by Mr. " *Speaker*; and that the House expecteth it to be done, and to hear " by *Monday* next that this be done; and in the mean Time, the " House will respite any Resolution concerning themselves; and that " they attend the House again on *Monday* Morning: And the like " Notice to be given to Mr. *Comptroller* and Sir *H. Martyn*, by " the Serjeant: All which was done by Mr. *Speaker* accordingly.

10 *June*, p. 869. " Sir *George More* informeth the House, That " he was present at a High Commission Court, where Seven Bishops " present; and knoweth, that there all the Proceedings against Sir " *Robert Howard*, from the 1st of *February*, 22 *Jac.* were frus- " trated and made void. And Sir *H. Martyn* affirmed, that the " Order of the House there read and allowed; and all ordered to " be done there accordingly.

" *Tuesday* next, for full Satisfaction to be given to this House, " of the Performance of the Order concerning Sir *Ro. Howard*."

On the 15th *June*, the Parliament was dissolved.

1661,

Appendix.
—(B.)—
Report 1771.

[23]

1661, 18 *December*, Vol. VIII. p. 335. Case of Sterling.

" Upon Information given to this House, That Alderman " *Sterling*, One of the Sheriffs of *London*, being served with an " Order, signed by Mr. *Speaker*, to discharge *James Lyde*, menial " Servant to Sir *Henry Herbert*, (who was arrested and imprisoned " in *The Poultry Compter*) out of Prison; the said Sheriff refused to " obey the said Order, or discharge the said *Lyde*; but put the " Order up in his Pocket, and said, he would answer it to the Speaker " in the House.

" Resolved, That the said Sheriff *Sterling* be forthwith this Morning " sent for, in Custody of the Serjeant at Arms, to this House, to an- " swer his Misdemeanor and Breach of Privilege."

Dec. 19. " Resolved, That Sheriff *Sterling* be called to the Bar " of this House; and shall, upon his Knees, receive the Reprehen- " sion of Mr. *Speaker*, for his Contempt and Breach of the Order " of this House; and that he be continued in the Custody of the " Serjeant at Arms, till he do cause *Lyde*, Servant to Sir *Henry Her- " bert*, to be released out of Prison, without any Fees or Charges.

" The Sheriff being called in, and kneeling at the Bar, Mr. " *Speaker* gave him a grave Reprehension; and told him, That some " Sheriffs of *London*, for a less Offence, had been sent to *The Tower*; " but, in regard of his loyal Affections to His Majesty, the House " was pleased to remit his Offence, upon the Enlargement of the " Prisoner: But that he should remain in the Serjeant's Custody " until the Prisoner was released, as aforesaid."

---

4 *June*, 1675, P. M. Vol. IX. p. 353. " Ordered, That Mr. " *Speaker* do issue out a Warrant to *John Topham* Esquire, Serjeant " at Arms now attending this House, to authorize and require him, " that if any Person or Persons shall attempt or go about to arrest, " Imprison, or detain him from executing his Office, or from his " Attendance upon this House, to apprehend such Persons, and " bring them in Custody to answer their Breach of Privilege; and " to require and authorize all Persons to be aiding and assisting to " him therein."

4th *June*, 1689, Vol. X. p. 164. " A Petition of *John Topham* " Esquire was read; setting forth, That he, being a Serjeant at " Arms, and attending the House, in the Years 1679 and 1680, " when several Orders were made and directed to the Petitioner, for " the taking into his Custody the several Persons of Sir *Charles Neal*, " &c. &c. and others, for several Misdemeanors by them com-

 " mitted,

Appendix
—(B.)—
Report 1771.

[24]

" mitted, in Breach of the Privilege of the House; and, after that " the Commons were dissolved, the said Persons, being resolved to " ruin the Petitioner, did, in *Hilary Term*, the 33d or 34th of King " *Charles*   , sue the Petitioner in the King's Bench, in several " Actions of Trespass, Battery, and false Imprisonment, for taking " and detaining them as aforesaid: To which Actions the Petitioner " pleaded to the Jurisdiction of the Court the said several Orders; " but such his Plea was overruled; the then Judges ruling the Pe- " titioner to plead in Chief, and thereupon he pleaded the Orders " in Bar to the Actions; notwithstanding which Plea and Orders, " the then Judges gave Judgement against him, &c."

5th *July*, p. 209. " Colonel *Birch* reports from the Committee " of Privileges and Elections, to whom the Petition of *J. Topham* " was referred, &c.

" Whereupon the House Resolved, That this House doth agree " with the Committee, That the Judgement given by the Court of " King's Bench, *Easter Term*, 34 *Car*. II. Regis, upon the Plea of " *John Topham*, at the Suit of *John Jay*, to the Jurisdiction of that " Court; and also the Judgements given against the said Mr. *Topham*, " at the Suit of *Samuel Verdon*, &c. are Illegal, and a Violation of " the Privileges of Parliament, and pernicious to the Rights of " Parliament.

" Ordered, That Sir *Francis Pemberton*, Sir *Thomas Jones*, and Sir " *Francis Wythers*, do attend this House, on *Wednesday* Morning " next."

19 *July*, p. 227. " Sir *Francis Pemberton* and Sir *Thomas Jones* " attending, were called in; and having been heard in their De- " fence, were committed to the Serjeant at Arms, for their Breach " of Privileges of this House, by giving Judgement to over-rule the " Plea, to the Jurisdiction of the Court of King's Bench, in the " Case between *Jay* and *Topham*."

The Case of Sir *William Williams*, against whom, after the Dissolution of the Parliament held at *Oxford*, an Information was brought, by the Attorney General, in the King's Bench, in *Trin. Term*, 36 *Car*. IIdi, for a Misdemeanor, for having printed the Information against *Thomas Dangerfield*, which he had ordered to be printed, when he was Speaker, by Order of the House. Judgement passed against him on this Information in the Second Year of King *James* the Second.——This Proceeding the Convention Parliament deemed so great a Grievance, and so high an Infringement of the Rights of Parliament, that it appears to your Committee to be the principal, if not the sole, Object of the First Part of the Eighth

[25]

Eighth Head of the Means used by King *James* to subvert the Laws and Liberties of this Kingdom, as set forth in the Declaration of the Two Houses; which will appear evident from the Account given in the Journal, 8th *Feb.* 1688, of the forming of that Declaration, the Eighth Head of which was at first conceived in these Words; *videlicet*, "By causing Informations to be brought "and prosecuted in the Court of King's Bench, for Matters and "Causes cognizable only in Parliament; and by divers other arbi-"trary and illegal Courses."

11 *February*, 1688. "To this Article the Lords disagreed; and "gave for a Reason, Because they do not fully apprehend what "is meant by it, nor what Instances there have been of it; which "therefore they desire may be explained, if the House shall think "fit to insist further on it."

12 *February*, 1688. "The House disagree with the Lords in their "Amendment of leaving out the Eighth Article. But in respect of "the Liberty given by the Lords in explaining that Matter;

"Resolved, That the Words do stand in this Manner:

"By Prosecutions in the Court of King's Bench for Matters "and Causes cognizable only in Parliament, and by divers "other arbitrary and illegal Courses."

By which Amendment, your Committee observes, that the House adapted the Article more correctly to the Case they had in View; for the Information was filed in King *Charles* the Second's Time; but the Prosecution was carried on, and Judgment obtained, in the Second Year of King *James*.

That the Meaning of the House should be made more evident to the Lords; the House Ordered, "That Sir *William Williams* be "added to the Managers of the Conference;" and Sir *William Williams* the same Day reports the Conference with the Lords; and, "That their Lordships had adopted the Article in the Words as "amended by the Commons." And corresponding to this Article of Grievance, is the Assertion of the Right of the Subject, in the Ninth Article of the Declaratory Part of the Bill of Rights; *videlicet*, "That the Freedom and Debates or Proceedings in Par-"liament ought not to be impeached or questioned in any Court or "Place out of Parliament."

To which may be added, the latter Part of the Sixth Resolution of the Exceptions to be made in the Bill of Indemnity, Journal, Vol. X. p. 146, wherein, after reciting the Surrender of Charters, and the Violating the Rights and Freedoms of Elections,

I &c.

&c. it proceeds in these Words: "And the questioning the "Proceedings of Parliament, out of Parliament, by Declarations, "Informations, or otherwise, are Crimes for which some Persons "may be justly excepted out of the Bill of Indemnity."

On the 11th of *June*, 1689, p. 177. "The House Ordered, That "the Records of the Court of King's Bench, relating to the "Proceedings against *William Williams* Esquire, now Sir *William* "*Williams*, Knight and Baronet, late Speaker of this House, be "brought into this House, by the *Custos Brevium* of the said Court, "on *Thursday* Morning next."

On the 12th of *July*, p. 215, "The Record was read; and the "House thereupon Resolved, That the Judgement given in the "Court of King's Bench, in *Easter Term*, 2 *Jac.* IIdi, against *Wil-* "*liam Williams* Esquire, Speaker of the House of Commons, in the "Parliament held at *Westminster*, 25 *October*, 32 *Car.* IIdi, for "Matters done by Order of the House of Commons, and as Speaker "thereof, is an illegal Judgement, and against the Freedom of Par- "liament.

"Resolved, That a Bill be brought in, to reverse the said Judge- "ment."

This Bill was Twice read; but went no further in that Session.

1691, 28 *April*, Vol. X. p. 537. "A Complaint being made "to the House, That *Sam. Hughes* and *William Phillipps*, Esquires, "*Walter Thornborough*, an Attorney at Law, and *Francis Meare*, "had, by a Prosecution at Law in the last Great Session for the "County of *Pembroke*, endeavoured to turn *Richard* Viscount "*Bulkeley* of the Kingdom of *Ireland*, a Member of this House, "out of the Possession of Part of his Estate;

"Ordered, That it be referred to Mr. *Speaker*, &c.

"Ordered, That Mr. *Speaker* do write a Letter to the Prothono- "tary that he do not take out, and to the Sheriff of the County "of *Pembroke* that he do not execute, any Writ, whereby the Lord "*Bulkeley's* Possession may be disturbed, until Mr. *Speaker* shall "have examined and reported the Matter to the House, and this "House take further Order therein."

1716, *April* 13, 14, 16, Vol. XVIII. p. 420. "The House being "acquainted, that *Jonathan Elford* Esquire, a Member of this House, "has been summoned, by *John Metcalf* and *Alexander Ward*, Esquires, "Two Justices of the Peace for the County of *Middlesex*, to appear "before them, to take the Oaths appointed by the late Act of Par- "liament; which Summons was delivered in at the Clerk's Table, "and read:

"Ordered,

Appendix
—(B.)—
Report 1771.

[27]

" Ordered, That *John Metcalf* and *Alexander Ward*, Esquires, do attend this House To-morrow Morning."

April 14. " Were called in: They acknowledged they did issue a Warrant for Mr. *Elford* to come and take the Oaths; but that they did not know he was a Member of the House until they had made a Return into the Quarter Sessions.

" Ordered, That the Clerk of the Peace for the County of *Middlesex* do attend, upon *Monday* Morning next, with the Return, &c.

April 16, " Ordered, *Nem. Con.* That the Deputy Clerk of the Peace for the County of *Middlesex* be called in, and, at the Table, erase the name of *Jonathan Elford* Esquire, a Member of this House, out of the Return made by *John Metcalf* and *Alexander Ward*, Esquires, Two of the Justices of the Peace for the said County, of such Persons as have been summoned by them to take the Oaths, and who have neglected and refused so to do.

" And Mr. *Hardesty* was called in; and, at the Table, erased out the Name of *Jonathan Elford* accordingly."

---

14 *Nov.* 1640, 2 Vol. p. 29. " Ordered, That a Warrant shall issue, under Mr. *Speaker's* Hand, to all Mayors, Justices of Peace, Bailiffs, Sheriffs, Constables, and other His Majesty's Officers of this Kingdom, requiring them to be assistant to the Bearer or Bearers of the Warrant of this House, for the bringing in safe Custody Sir *G. Radcliffe* to this House, for the better and more effectual Execution of his or their said Warrant."

January 11th, 1641, Vol. II. p. 371. " Ordered, That, in the Execution of the Warrant of this House for the apprehending of Sir *Basil Brooke*, the Serjeant at Arms attending this House, his Deputy or Deputies, do require the Assistance of all Sheriffs, Justices of Peace, Constables, and other Officers, for the apprehending of the said Sir *Basil Brooke*; and to use all possible Diligence herein."

---

21 *December* 1660, Vol. VIII. p. 222. " This House having formerly issued an Order for the Serjeant at Arms, &c. to send for in Custody *William Nabbs* and Mr. *Maurice Thompson*, for violating the Privilege of this House, in the Case of Sir *Francis Lawley*; and being informed that the said *Nabbs* withdrawn himself; and that the Serjeant's Deputies, who had in Charge the Warrant as to Mr. *Thompson*, were denied Admittance to him; and that slighting and contemptuous Words were given touching the Warrant; the said Deputies were called in to the Bar of this House, and examined, *videlicet*, *Walter Curtis* and *Simon Lowe*.

I 2 " Resolved,

"Resolved, That Mr. *Maurice Tompson* be sent for, in Custody, as a Delinquent; and that the Serjeant at Arms be empowered to break open Mr. *Tompson's* House in case of Resistance, and also to bring in Custody all such as shall make Opposition therein; and he is to call to his Assistance the Sheriff of *Middlesex*, and all other Officers as he shall see Cause, who are required to assist him accordingly."

January 24, 1670, Vol. IX. p. 193. "Information being given of a very high Contempt and Misdemeanor committed against the House, by assaulting and beating *George Dudley*, Deputy to the Serjeant at Arms, and rescuing out of his Custody *Thomas Parsons*, &c.

"Which Misdemeanor and Rescue, the said *Dudley* did testify, was committed by Mr. *John Cox*, Under Sheriff of the County of *Gloucester*, and his Bailiff and others.

"Resolved, That the Serjeant at Arms attending this House, or such Deputy or Deputies as he shall appoint, do apprehend and take into Custody Mr. *John Cox*, Under Sheriff of the County of *Gloucester*, *William Forder*, &c. &c. &c.

"And the High Sheriff of the County of *Gloucester*, and other Officers concerned, are to be required, by Warrant from Mr. *Speaker*, to be aiding and assisting in the Execution of such Warrant."

Vide also—*Topham*, as before, *June* 4, 1675, P. M.

---

26 *February* 1701, Vol. XIII. p. 767. "Resolved, That to assert, the House of Commons have no Power of Commitment, but of their own Members, tends to the Subversion of the Constitution of the House of Commons."

MINUTES OF EVIDENCE.

LIST OF WITNESSES.

Mercurii, 22° die Februarii, 1837.

MEMBERS PRESENT.

Sir William Follett.
Lord Viscount Howick.
Sir Robert Harry Inglis, Bart.
Sir Frederick Pollock.
Mr. Roebuck.
Lord Stanley.
Mr. Tancred.
Mr. C. Villiers.
Mr. Serjeant Wilde.
The Right Hon. C. W. Williams Wynn.

LORD VISCOUNT HOWICK, IN THE CHAIR.

Mr. *Thomas Gurney*, called in; and Examined.

Mr. Thos. Gurney.
22 February 1837.

1. *Chairman.*] DID you take a short-hand note of the proceedings in the case of Stockdale v. Hansard, in the Court of King's Bench, on the 7th of February in this year?—I took a short-hand note of the summing-up of Lord Denman, and also of the latter part of the reply of the plaintiff. Mr. Oliver, our assistant, took a note of the former part of the case.

2. Are the notes of that part of the case which was taken by you a correct report of what passed?—They are.

Mr. *William Oliver*, called in; and Examined.

Mr. Wm. Oliver.

3. *Chairman.*] DID you take the report of the commencement of the trial of Stockdale v. Hansard, on the 7th of February last?—I did.

4. You reported the proceedings up to the place where Mr. Thomas Gurney commences his report?—I did.

5. Are these accurate copies of your notes?—[*handing to the Witness a transcript of part of the proceedings on the trial.*]—Yes, they are. I have examined them with the original short-hand notes. [*The Witness delivered in the same.*]

6. Is that an accurate statement of the proceedings that took place at the trial?—It is.

7. Mr. *Serjeant Wilde.*] Just mark the part where your note concludes?—It terminates at the bottom of page 118.

Jovis, 23° die Februarii, 1837.

MEMBERS PRESENT.

Mr. Attorney-General.	Sir Geo. Strickland, Bart.
Sir George Clerk, Bart.	Mr. Tancred.
Lord Viscount Howick.	Mr. Serjeant Wilde.
Sir R. H. Inglis, Bart.	The Right Hon. C. W. Williams Wynn.
Sir Robert Peel, Bart.	

LORD VISCOUNT HOWICK IN THE CHAIR.

Sir *Archer Croft*, called in; and Examined.

Sir *Archer Croft*.

23 February 1837.

8. Mr. *Attorney-General*.] YOU are clerk of Nisi Prius in the Court of King's Bench?—I am.

9. Were you officiating as clerk at Nisi Prius upon the trial of the case of Stockdale v. Hansard?—Yes, I was.

10. Have you brought with you a copy of the minutes of the verdict?—Yes, I have.

11. Will you hand it in?—

[*The Witness delivered in the same, which was read, as follows:*]

"Middlesex. Tuesday 7th of February 1837.

"Sittings after Hilary Term. Before the Right Honourable Lord Denman.

"Stockdale v. Hansard and others.

"1st Issue - - - - - Plaintiff.
"2d Issue - - - - - Defendants.

"The above is a true copy of the minute of the verdict returned by the jury in that case.

(signed) "*A. D. Croft*,
"Clk. Ni. Pr. K. B."

"23d February 1837.

Mr. *Richard Preston*, called in; and Examined.

Mr. *R. Preston*.

12. Mr. *Attorney-General*.] YOU acted as attorney for the defendants in the cause of Stockdale v. Hansard?—Yes, in conjunction with Mr. Parkes.

13. Have you the proceedings in that case?—I have a portion of them with me.

14. Have you the declaration?—Yes.

15. Have you the plea as it was originally drawn?—Yes.

16. With the rule to plead several matters?—Yes.

17. Originally, was there a plea of not guilty; and then a plea justifying under the orders of the House of Commons; and thirdly, a plea justifying that the publication of Mr. Stockdale was of the character imputed to it?—Yes.

18. How was it that those pleas were altered?—When you plead several matters, it is necessary to have a judge's order; and accordingly I attended before Mr. Justice Littledale, in order to have his order to that effect; and Mr. Justice Littledale, on reading the pleas, said that he did not think he could admit the three, but that he would allow either the first and the third, or the second and the third; but he would not allow the general issue, the second plea, stating that it was by order of the House of Commons; but he said that he would consider it, and desired me to come the next day.

19. Was there any opposition made on the part of the plaintiff to your having leave to plead these three pleas?—None whatever.

20. Was it merely the suggestion of the judge himself?—It was; although we had given notice to the opposite attorney of our intention to appear before the judge to apply for several matters.

21. Then he took to the following day to consider?—He did. On the following day I attended, and he repeated his objection, and said that I had better tell my counsel that he objected to the three pleas, and ask them what they had to say in support of the three; I accordingly waited upon Mr. Crompton, the junior counsel,

Mr. B. Preston.

13 February 1837.

counsel, who had settled the pleas, and stated to him what Mr. Justice Littledale had stated with regard to the three pleas; and Mr. Crompton said that, in his opinion, the judge was right, but that it would be well if we could get the three admitted. I accordingly went before Mr. Justice Littledale again, and stated to him that I had mentioned his objection to counsel, and that counsel still thought it advisable to get the three pleas allowed. Mr. Justice Littledale remarked that he could not agree with counsel, and he should accordingly strike out the second plea, which he did; and the order was then drawn up to plead the first and third pleas.

22. You went to trial with two pleas; one, not guilty, and the second justifying that the publication was indecent and disgusting?—Exactly. I ought to observe that Mr. Justice Littledale stated, when he declined allowing the second plea, that it was a plea which would arise under the general issue.

23. You would have an opportunity of giving in defence that evidence, under the plea of not guilty?—Yes.

24. Have you a copy of the record?—No; we applied for it, and they stated that as we did not take it, the plaintiff must have taken it.

25. Have you a copy of the issue?—No, I have not; I am unable to find it.

26. Mr. Serjeant *Wilde*.] You have a copy of the declaration, and of your own pleas?—Yes, I have; I have with me the draft declaration, the draft pleas, the draft replication, and the draft rejoinder.

(*The Witness delivered in the same*)—vide Appendix.

27. Mr. *Attorney-General*.] How did you come to be concerned as attorney for the defendants in the action?—I do not know further than that Messrs. Hansard generally have our printing.

28. Had you any communication upon the subject with the printer of the House of Commons?—None; Mr. Hansard came to us; it was at the time when Parliament was not sitting, in October, and stated that he had received notice from Mr. Stockdale that he was going to commence an action against him, and that he had been requested to name his attorneys, and he should be glad to know if we would undertake the conduct of his defence.

29. Then you acted merely upon the private retainer of Messrs. Hansard?—We did.

30. Mr. Serjeant *Wilde*.] Did the Judge take upon himself to strike out the particular plea which you have mentioned, or leave it to you to select which of the two you would have out of the three?—The judge gave us our option.

31. And you elected to take the first and the third pleas?—Yes.

32. It was open to you to take either the first and the third pleas, or the first and the second, and you elected to take the first and the third?—Yes, we did, under the advice of counsel, of course.

Jovis, 2° die Martii, 1837.

MEMBERS PRESENT.

Mr. Attorney-General.	Lord Stanley.
Sir George Clerk.	Sir George Strickland.
Sir William Follett.	Mr. Tancred.
Lord Viscount Howick.	Mr. Charles Villiers.
Sir Robert H. Inglis.	Mr. Serjeant Wilde.
Sir Robert Peel.	Mr. C. W. Williams Wynn.
Sir Frederick Pollock.	

LORD VISCOUNT HOWICK, IN THE CHAIR.

Luke Graves Hansard, Esq., called in; and Examined.

Luke G. Hansard, Esq.

2 March 1837.

33. *Chairman*.] YOU are Printer to the House of Commons?—I am, jointly with my Brother and our Sons.

34. You have some Papers relating to the publication of the Parliamentary Papers?—I have. In furtherance of the directions of The Speaker, search was made by me in the Library of the British Museum; and one of the papers is a

Luke G. Hansard, Esq.

2 March 1837.

"Statement of the Particulars relating to the Publishing and Sale of Votes and Parliamentary Papers, from the earliest period of record," being the result of the examination of the earliest Votes, commencing with 1641 and extending to 1777, with notices of several entries in the Journals relating to the subject. The other is a "Statement of the mode of Publication and Circulation from 1731 to 1836," when the sale commenced as authorised by the Resolution of the House of 13 August 1835.

35. Sir *R. H. Inglis.*] From what collection did you extract those particulars?—The earliest are from a collection of tracts on political and other controversial subjects, presented to the Museum by King George III.; the later facts, from the collection of Votes in the Library of the Museum. Those of the second period are collected from documents in our office.

[*The Papers were delivered in.*]

Resolved,

That the Chairman be directed to apply to the House that the Committee have liberty to report their proceedings, together with their opinion, to the House, and that the Petition of Messrs. Hansard, presented 6th February, be referred to the Committee.

Jovis, 23° die Martii, 1837.

MEMBERS PRESENT.

Lord Viscount Howick.
Sir Robert H. Inglis.
Mr. Tancred.
Mr. Serjeant Wilde.
Mr. C. W. Williams Wynn.

LORD VISCOUNT HOWICK, IN THE CHAIR.

Luke Graves Hansard, Esq., called in; and Examined.

Luke G. Hansard, Esq.

23 March 1837.

36. Mr. Serjeant *Wilde.*] IN the Paper presented by you to the Committee, in paragraph 15, you refer to certain Parliamentary Papers having the expression "printed and published" upon them. What are the Papers to which you refer?—To many in the Collection of Tracts in the Library of the House of Commons, formerly in the Speaker's Gallery. In volume 21 of these is a Declaration of the House of Commons, in 1641, expressed to be "printed and published." Likewise, in volumes 51 and 53, and in several others of the Collection, there are many Parliamentary Papers of the date of 1642, which have printed on them the order to be "forthwith printed and published," with a notification of being sold. Volume 76, in 1660, contains the King's letter and Declaration, and the letter of General Monck, and several other proceedings connected with the Restoration, which have the expression, "to be forthwith printed and published." There is likewise, in the same volume, the examinations of Bedlow and Dangerfield, with the Speaker's appointment and authority for printing in the usual way. In vol. 6, of 1667, is a book of rates, with the order for printing, and "to be forthwith published," signed by William Jessop, Clerk of the House of Commons. In volume 82, 1680, are the Papers about the Popish Plot, which, by entry in the Journals, is committed to the care of Mr. Treby. These have the appointment of the printer by Mr. Treby, as deputed by the Order of the House. In volume 74, 1704 to 1727, are the Articles of Union with Scotland, which are ordered to be "forthwith printed and published," and the title page has the bookseller's notice "to be sold." The volume of Votes, from 1680 to 1681, presented to the Library by Mr. Williams Wynn, has many instances of the appointment and authority of printing by The Speaker, with an advertisement for the sale of the Votes and Papers printed with them. Volumes 1 and 2, of the early collection of the Reports of the House of Commons, from 1744 to 1800, contain on the title pages generally, the expression, "Published by Order of the House." The first volume contains the Report of 1771, upon the Obstruction of the Orders of the House, which has already been laid before the Committee, and printed in fac-simile, and which, as far as my search has extended and my belief likewise, is the last instance of the kind.

37. In

Luke G. Hansard, Esq.

23 March 1837.

37. In page 5, of the Papers presented by you, it is stated that the expense of transmission of large packets of Parliamentary Proceedings is paid by the Government; what is the authority for that statement?—We have been in the habit, for these 30 years, of occasionally circulating the volumes of all important statistical facts to the public libraries and clerks of the peace, and other official authorities interested in them; and as those volumes have been too large and liable to injury, if transmitted by the post, they have been sent in packing cases, or any other convenient form, and the carriage paid at the cost of the public, charged by us in our account. The latest instance of that kind is the circulation of the volumes of the Population Abstracts, the last census that was taken, and which were so circulated very extensively.

38. The same Paper states the circulation of Papers in great numbers; are those statements made upon your own knowledge?—Certainly; the business has been transacted under our direction and by our servants.

39. Does your bill specify the numbers?—Certainly. When any subjects have been under discussion in Parliament, which greatly interested the public, either of Legislative or Commercial importance, such as the Municipal Reports, the Bills for establishing new forms of Municipal Constitutions, the Poor Law Reports and Bills, and several others of that kind, either generally concerning the community, or relating to laws particularly affecting local interests, they have been generally or locally circulated to a great extent; sometimes to all the clerks of the peace, the sheriffs, magistrates and corporate bodies, throughout the kingdom, as well as the public libraries.

Martis, 4° die Aprilis, 1837.

MEMBERS PRESENT.

Mr. Attorney-General.	Mr. Tancred.
Lord Viscount Howick.	Mr. Serjeant Wilde.
Sir Robert H. Inglis.	Mr. C. W. Williams Wynn.
Sir Robert Peel.	

LORD VISCOUNT HOWICK, IN THE CHAIR.

Sir Henry Ellis, called in; and Examined.

Sir Henry Ellis.

4 April 1837.

40. ARE you Principal Librarian in the British Museum?—I am.

41. Have you brought from the King's Collection of Pamphlets any and what volumes?—I produce four volumes of the collection, called The King's Pamphlets, consisting of papers and tracts printed between 1640 and 1660, given to the British Museum by King George the Third in 1763; also volumes of the Votes of the House of Commons, published from 1689 to 1732. The last-mentioned volumes are found in the old Library of the British Museum.

Luke Graves Hansard, Esq., called in; and Examined.

Luke G. Hansard, Esq.

42. HAVE you referred to the volumes now produced by Sir Henry Ellis, and can you point out the publications referred to in your former statements to the Committee?—My attention was directed by The Speaker to getting a knowledge of all facts relating to the terms in which the orders for printing were made, and the mode of publication and sale, from the earliest times of Parliamentary Printing to the present day. The Journals afford correct information of the terms in which the orders are made, but contain none as to the practice of sale, although there is frequent use of expressions to be "printed and published," and "published in print." The mode of publication and sale could only be learnt from an inspection of the Papers as actually printed and circulated. For obtaining this Information, the collection of tracts, formerly in The Speaker's Gallery, and now in the Library of the House, has been carefully looked over, and many particulars have been collected, some of which are referred to in my last evidence, and others are stated in a Paper before the Committee. But the greatest number have been gathered from the collection of pamphlets, some few volumes of which are now produced by Sir H. Ellis, in the years 1640 to 1643. On a great many of these, in volumes 1, 2, 3, the order for printing and publishing, and the notice of sale, are

See Paper of Statements, App. No. 3.

Luke G. Hansard, Esq.

4 April 1837.

are printed. Those in volume 5 show a variety of ways of publication as well as by sale. Volume 18 contains the orders and resolutions at the Restoration in 1660. The examination of the collection of Votes in the Museum, in continuation of Mr. Wynn's volume of 1680–81, show a continuation of the practice of notifying the Votes for Sale down to 1802, and a great number have the price printed on them. My particular attention was directed to the question of the Sale of Reports and Parliamentary Papers and Documents at an early period. The examination of this collection gives the answer to this question, for many Reports and Papers are bound up with the Votes. They all have printed on them the order of the House and The Speaker's Appointment of the Printer, with the words, in many instances, "Printed and Published by Order of the House." All have the bookseller's imprint; and the following Reports and Papers have the prices printed either on the title or last page. In 1711, Representation to The Queen, price 2*d.*; in the same year, The Speaker's Congratulatory Address to Mr. Harley on his escape from Assassination, price 2*d.*; in the same year, Report on Public Accounts, price 6*d.*; in the same year, Address to the Queen, price 1*d.*; in 1715, Report on Poor and Scavenger's Rate in Westminster, price 4*d.*; in 1730, List of Attornies, price 3*s.*; in 1732, Report on the Charitable Corporation, price 5*s.*; in the same year, Report on the Cottonian Library, price 5*s.*; in the same year, a list of Officers and Fees in the Court of King's Bench, price 6*d.*

APPENDIX

TO THE

MINUTES OF EVIDENCE.

LIST OF APPENDIX.

Appendix, No. 1.

EXTRACTS from the CASE of *Stockdale* v. *Hansard*, in the COURT of KING'S BENCH.

Mr. *Attorney-General*:—

NOW having admitted the publication, and having admitted that it referred to Mr. Stockdale, unless I have a defence, the verdict will be for the plaintiff; but I will state to you the defence I propose to lay before you.

Gentlemen, there are two. My lord will observe there is a plea of not guilty, and there is a justification that the work deserves the character ascribed to it in this report. Under the plea of not guilty Mr. Justice Littledale, on the authority of some recently decided cases, stated, that the first defence I have to offer was to be given in evidence; and he struck out the special plea, because he said, according to the rules of pleading, we were not entitled to it, there being the general issue. My first defence is, that Messrs. Hansard acted in strict accordance with the orders of the House of Commons. It is an action, in fact, brought against a servant of the House of Commons.

Lord *Denman*.—I understand it was purchased.

Mr. *Attorney-General*.—Yes, my lord; I will show exactly how that was. It was purchased in Abingdon-street, where the sale goes on under the authority of Parliament. I shall state the facts as they are.

Lord *Denman*.—I doubt whether there can be any privilege to sell libels.

Mr. *Attorney-General*.—I am going to state the facts, and your lordship will either decide the law ——

Lord *Denman*.—If it had been merely written or printed for the use of the Members, it would be a different thing.

Mr. *Attorney-General*.—I am going to state the orders of the House, and it is thought by persons of the highest Parliamentary experience in this country, that this authority is a clear defence. I was going to state that an Act passed in the 4th and 5th years of His present Majesty, intituled "An Act for effecting greater uniformity of practice in the government of the several Prisons in England and Wales, and for appointing Inspectors of Prisons in Great Britain." Gentlemen, by the 7th section of that Act it is enacted, "That it shall be lawful for one of His Majesty's principal Secretaries of State to nominate and appoint a sufficient number of fit and proper persons, not exceeding five, to visit and inspect, either singly or together, every gaol, bridewell, house of correction, penitentiary, or other prison or

392. t. place

Appendix, No. 1.

Stockdale v. Hansard.

Extracts from Attorney-General's Defence.

place kept or used for the confinement of prisoners in any part of the kingdom of Great Britain; and every person so appointed shall have authority to examine any person holding any office, or receiving any salary or emolument in any such gaol, bridewell, house of correction, penitentiary, prison, or other place of confinement as aforesaid; and to call for and inspect all books and papers relating thereto, and to inquire into all matters touching and concerning such gaol, bridewell, house of correction, penitentiary, prison, or other place of confinement; and every such person so appointed shall, on or before the 1st day of February in every year, make a separate and distinct report in writing of the state of every gaol, bridewell, house of correction, penitentiary, prison, or other place of confinement visited by him; and shall transmit the same to one of His Majesty's principal Secretaries of State, and a copy of every such Report shall be laid before both Houses of Parliament within 14 days after such 1st day of February if they shall be then assembled, or if Parliament shall not be then assembled, within 14 days after the meeting thereof after such 1st day of February."

Gentlemen, under this Act inspectors were appointed, Mr. Crawford and Mr. Russell, for the metropolitan district; they inspected, amongst other gaols, the gaol of Newgate, and they made a Report, which was laid before the Parliament under the statute I have read to you; that Report was laid before the House of Commons, and ordered to be printed the 22d of March 1836, and this is the Report which Mr. Stockdale alleges to be a libel. Now, my lord has intimated an opinion that if this had been merely printed for the use of the Members of the House it would be no libel, because it is a Parliamentary proceeding; and the court would take judicial notice——

Lord *Denman*.—It is a statutable proceeding after that.

Mr. *Attorney-General*.—It is even a statutable proceeding. His lordship will recollect the case of Lake v. King, which occurred in the time of Charles II., and which was decided by Lord Hale and the rest of the judges. There the court held that the printing of a petition, though it reflected upon the plaintiff, was no libel, and no action could be maintained. Now, what I have to show is, that though this was bought by the plaintiff's son at this house in Abingdon-street; that it is protected, and has the same privilege.

Gentlemen, there was a Resolution of the House of Commons on the 13th of August 1835, in these words: "Resolved, That the Parliamentary Papers and Reports printed for the use of the House should be rendered accessible to the public by purchase, at the lowest price they can be furnished, and that a sufficient number of extra copies shall be printed for that purpose." That was in the Session of 1835. Then, in the Session of 1836, these Resolutions passed, Friday, March the 18th, 1836: "That the Parliamentary Papers and Reports, and also the Votes and Appendix to the Votes should be sold to the public at the price of one half-penny per sheet. That all Charts, Plans or drawings which these Papers may contain be charged at the rate of 3 d. for each half sheet, of 6 d. for each whole sheet, of foolscap size, and 1 s. per sheet of larger size. That papers of former Sessions, now remaining in store, be sold at the same rate as those of the current Session. That Messrs. Hansard, the Printers to the House, be appointed to conduct the sale. That, in order to render the Parliamentary Papers accessible to the public through the means of other booksellers, it is expedient that a discount of 25 per cent. should be allowed to the trade who shall become purchasers. That the Committee recommend that Messrs. Hansard should charge in their accounts the actual expense incurred by them in carrying on the sale as proposed in these Resolutions."

Gentlemen, these Resolutions being passed, Messrs. Hansards have acted in strict conformity to the Orders of the House; they have sold the Reports, and have sold them without any profit; they had no interest whatever in the sale of them; they are the mere instruments of the House: in fact, they are the servants and agents of the House, and this is an action against the House of Commons.

Now, upon these facts I humbly submit to my lord that, under the plea of Not Guilty, we are entitled to a verdict, if we are entitled to it at all; that is the proper plea. This is repelling the charge of malice, and not guilty is the proper plea under which it is to be given in evidence. I submit, when we show that this publication took place in conformity to the express orders of the House of Commons, we are privileged, and it cannot be considered a libel.

Gentlemen, I will remind my lord of the case of The King v. Wright, which went a great deal farther. In that case Lord Kenyon, and the other judges of the Court of King's Bench who assisted him, declared that not only the bookseller or printer who printed or published a work in conformity to the order of the House of Commons were exempted from any action or prosecution for a libel, but that that could not be considered a libel which the House of Commons had ordered to be published; and although Wright was not the printer of the House of Commons, nor acted under their orders; although he re-printed a Report that the House of Commons had printed by its own printer, the Court of King's Bench decided that this publication, which had been authorized originally by the House of Commons, could not be considered a libel. I will just remind his lordship of what Lord Kenyon says; but before I go to that, I will say that the only authority on the other side is the case of Sir William Williams, shortly before the Revolution: he being the Speaker of the House, by the order of the House he directed Dangerfield's Narrative to be published; a prosecution was instituted against him, and I must say that the judges of that day illegally and corruptly held that he was guilty; but that judgment has been repudiated, and after that time those judges were called to account for their illegal decision; but, except that, I know of no case in which it has been held that a person, acting in obedience to the orders of the House of Commons, has been called in question for publishing any thing printed by order of the House of Commons. Now you shall hear what Lord Kenyon says: "When the motion was first made, I suggested

to

Appendix, No. 1.

Stockdale v. Hansard.

Extracts from Attorney-General's Defence.

to the counsel for the prosecutor, that if the publication in question really were what it professed to be, a copy of the Report of the House of Commons, it would be wrong to grant a rule to show cause; but it not being then admitted to be a true copy, and it being contended that the publication assumed a title that did not belong to it, we granted a rule nisi; but as it now proves to be a true copy of the Report, I think there was not the least pretence for the motion. This is an application for leave to file a criminal information against the defendant for publishing a libel, so that the application supposes that the publication is a libel. But the inquiry made by the House of Commons was an inquisition taken by one branch of the Legislature to enable them to proceed further, and adopt some regulations for the better government of the country. This Report was first made by a Committee of the House of Commons, then approved by the House at large, and then communicated to the other House, and it is now *sub judice*, and yet it is said that this is a libel on the prosecutor. It is impossible for us to admit that the proceeding of either of the Houses of Parliament is a libel, and yet that is to be taken as the foundation of this application. The case of Rex v. Sir W. Williams, which was principally relied upon, happened in the worst of times, but it has no relation to the present case. There the publication was the paper of a private individual, and, under pretence of the sanction of the House of Commons, an individual published; but this is a proceeding by one branch of the Legislature, and therefore we cannot inquire into it. I do not say that cases may not be put in which we would not inquire whether or not the House of Commons were justified in any particular measure; if, for instance, they were to send their Serjeant-at-arms to arrest a counsel here who was arguing a case between two individuals, or to grant an injunction to stay the proceedings here in a common action, undoubtedly we should pay no attention to it. But the report in question being adopted by the House at large is a proceeding of those who by the constitution are the guardians of the liberties of the subject, and we cannot say that any part of that proceeding is a libel." That is the doctrine laid down by Lord Kenyon, adopted by Mr. Justice Grose, Mr. Justice Lawrence, and, I think, by Mr. Justice Le Blanc. The present Report, which Mr. Stockdale represents as a libel, is laid before the House of Commons in pursuance of the Act; it is ordered to be printed by the House of Commons; and the House ordered it to be sold by Mr. Hansard for the information of the public. Under these circumstances it is the act of the House itself, and this distinguishes it from the cases that may be passing in my lord's mind—The King v. Lord Abingdon and The King v. Creevy. It was held that Lord Abingdon having made a speech in the House reflecting most severely upon the character of some person, though he was privileged in his place in Parliament, he was not justified in publishing it to the world. Again it was held in Creevy's case, that having made a speech in Parliament, he could not be questioned for what he said in his place in Parliament; but that having voluntarily, without the sanction of the House, published what he represented as his speech, and that being libellous upon individuals, he had no right to publish it, but there Mr. Creevy was not acting by the Order of the House, he did it merely voluntarily and as an individual. It was therefore held he was liable for the publication, because he was the author; and whether it was made in Parliament or out of Parliament was immaterial; but in the present case this is a work ordered to be printed by the House, ordered to be distributed by the House by Messrs. Hansard, and which they have distributed in obedience to the Orders of the House. I therefore submit to your Lordship, when I have made out, which I shall clearly do, that this was the mode of publication and that all notion of malice is repelled, that upon the plea of not guilty I am entitled to your verdict.

James Unige, Esq. sworn; Examined by Mr. *Attorney-General*.

You are clerk of the Journals of the House of Commons?—Yes.

Have you got the Journals; do you produce the order of the House for printing this Report?—I have got the original papers and the Report.

Just turn to the order for printing it.—[*The witness turned to the same.*]

The 22d of March 1836?—The 18th of March I have it. "Mr. Fox Maule also presented, pursuant to directions"—No, that will not do, that is not the right one.

Here it is "Ordered to be printed the 22d of March 1836?"—I do not find it under either of those dates.

Mr. *Attorney-General*.—It is ordered to be printed on that day; is there any doubt about it?

Plaintiff.—I do not mean to interpose any doubt.

Mr. *Attorney-General*.—Then it is admitted. Now turn to the 13th of August 1835.—Yes.

Read the resolution of that date?—There are several.

"Resolved, that the Parliamentary Papers and Reports printed for the use of the House should be rendered accessible to the public by purchase, at the lowest price they can be furnished, and that a sufficient number of extra copies shall be printed for that purpose." That is agreed to; now turn to the Resolutions of Friday, March 18, 1836?—There is an entry on the 18th March 1836; "Mr. Fox Maule presented, pursuant to directions"——

That is not it; I want the resolution respecting the printing and publishing of these papers.

Plaintiff.—I have no wish to interpose a difficulty; I will admit it with pleasure.

Lord *Denman*.—By the Resolution of the 13th of August 1835, it is merely that they should be sold, not that Messrs. Hansard should sell them.

Mr. *Attorney-General*.—Turn to the 18th March of 1836, which is likewise admitted, and according to that one of the Resolutions is, "That Messrs. Hansard, the printers to the House, be appointed to conduct the same." Very well, that closes that head. Now I propose to read one or two passages from this book. If there are any females, or any young persons in court, they had better retire.

Appendix, No. 1.

Stockdale v. Hansard.

Extract from Lord Denman's Charge.

EXTRACT from Lord *Denman's* Charge.

It seems to me, gentlemen, that the only questions for you upon the general issue can be, first, whether the publication was by the defendants at all; and, secondly, whether it is the publication of a libel; because on the third ground, namely, that this is a privileged publication, I am bound to say, as it comes before me as a question of law for my direction, that I entirely disagree from the law laid down by the learned counsel for the defendant. I am not aware of the existence in this country of any body whatever that can privilege any servant of theirs to publish libels of any individual. Whatever arrangements may be made between the House of Commons and any publisher in their employ, I am of opinion, that the publisher who publishes that in his public shop, and especially for money, which may be injurious, and possibly ruinous to any one of the King's subjects, must answer in a court of justice to that subject if he challenge him for a libel, and I wish to say so emphatically and distinctly, because I think that if, upon the first opportunity that arose in a court of justice for questioning that point, it were left unsatisfactorily explained, the judge who sat there might become an accomplice in the destruction of the liberties of the country, and expose every individual who lives in it to a tyranny that no man ought to submit to.

Gentlemen, I think that the case which has been quoted on that subject is not applicable to the present; it does not go the whole length, and it seems to me that it is not in any respect capable of being urged as an authority to prevent my going the length I have just now stated; therefore my direction to you, subject to a question hereafter, is, that the fact of the House of Commons having directed Messrs. Hansard to publish all their Parliamentary Reports, is no justification for them or for any bookseller who publishes a Parliamentary Report containing a libel against any man.

Appendix, No. 2.

COPIES of the Declaration, Plea, Replication and Rejoinder in the Case of *Stockdale* v. *Hansard*.

Stockdale v. *Hansard & Others*.—Declaration.

Appendix, No. 2.

Declaration.

In the King's Bench, the 7th day of November, in the year of our Lord 1836.

Middlesex to wit. JOHN JOSEPH STOCKDALE, the Plaintiff in this Suit, by Thomas Burton Howard, his attorney, complains of James Hansard, Luke Graves Hansard, Luke James Hansard and Luke Henry Hansard, the Defendants in this Suit, who have been summoned to answer the said John Joseph Stockdale in an action on the case: FOR that whereas, before and at the time of committing of the grievance next hereinafter complained of, he the said Plaintiff was and for a long space of time had been a bookseller and publisher of books, and as such bookseller and publisher had published divers and very many scientific and learned books, and particularly in the year of our Lord 1827, a certain physiological and anatomical book on the Generative System, illustrated with anatomical plates. Yet the said Defendants, well knowing the premises, but contriving and maliciously intending to defame and injure the said Plaintiff in his said trade of a bookseller and publisher, and to cause it to be believed that he published indecent and obscene books, on the 1st day of May in the year of our Lord 1836 maliciously did publish and cause to be published of and concerning the said Plaintiff in his said trade and business, in a certain book purporting to be "Reports of the Inspectors of Prisons of Great Britain," the false, scandalous, malicious and defamatory libel following, that is to say, "We also found several books: amongst them Guthrie's Grammar, a song book, the Keepsake Annual for 1836, and the ———, by ———, 10 plates, published by Stockdale, 1827. This last is a book of a most disgusting nature, and the plates are obscene and indecent in the extreme:" To the great injury of the said Plaintiff in his said trade and business, and also of his fair fame and reputation, and to the damage of the said Plaintiff of 800 *l*., and thereupon he brings Suit, &c.

John Joseph Stockdale
against
James Hansard,
Luke Graves Hansard,
Luke James Hansard,
and
Luke Henry Hansard.

Upon reading the Petition and Affidavit of the Plaintiff, and the certificate written at the foot of the said Petition, I order that the Plaintiff may sue as a poor person, and do assign him John Curwood, Esq., as his counsel, and Thomas Burton Howard, gentleman, as his attorney, according to the Prayer of the Petitioner.

Dated the 21st day of October 1836.

J. A. Park.

Appendix, No. 2.

Stockdale v. Hansard.

Declaration.

Stockdale v. Hansard & Others.

Let the Plaintiff's attorney or agent attend me at my chambers in Serjeant's Inn to-morrow, at three of the clock in the afternoon, to show cause why the Defendant should not have a month's time to plead in the Cause.

Dated the 8th day of November 1836. J. Patteson.

Stockdale v. Hansard & Others.

Upon hearing the attornies or agents on both sides, I do order that the Defendant shall have a week's time to plead, pleading issuably, rejoining gratis, and taking short notice of Trial, if necessary, for the third sitting in this Term.

Dated the 10th day of November 1836. J. Williams.

Stockdale v. Hansard & Others.

Upon hearing the attornies or agents on both sides, I do order that the Defendants shall have a week's time to plead, pleading issuably, rejoining gratis, and taking two days' notice of Trial if necessary, for the sittings after Term.

Dated 17th day of November 1836. J. Littledale.

Hansard & Others ats. Stockdale.—Plea.

In the King's Bench, the 22nd day of November, A. D. 1836.

Plea.

Hansard & Others ats. Stockdale.

The Defendants, by Joseph Parkes their attorney, say that they are not, nor are any, nor is either of them guilty of the grievances in the Declaration mentioned in manner and form as the Plaintiff hath above thereof complained against them; and of this the said Defendants put themselves upon the country, &c.: And for a further Plea in this behalf, the Defendants say that heretofore and before the commencement of this Suit, and after the making and passing of a certain Act of Parliament, holden at Westminster in the 5th & 6th years of the reign of our Sovereign Lord the now King, intituled "An Act for effecting greater uniformity of Practice in the Government of the several Prisons in Great Britain," to wit, on the 1st day of January A.D. 1836, The Right Hon. John Russell, Esq., (commonly called The Right Hon. Lord John Russell) then being one of His Majesty's Principal Secretaries of State, nominated and appointed William Crawford, Esq., and Whitworth Russell, Esq., to visit and inspect, either singly or together, every gaol, bridewell, house of correction, penitentiary or other prison or place kept for the confinement of prisoners in a certain part of Great Britain called the Home District: And afterwards and after the making of the said Act, and before the commencement of this Suit, and after the 1st day of February A. D. 1836, to wit, on the 1st day of March A. D. 1836, the said William Crawford and Whitworth Russell, under and by virtue of the said nomination and appointment, visited and inspected a certain gaol called Newgate Gaol, situate in the said part of Great Britain called the Home District, and did then find in the said gaol several books, and amongst those books Guthrie's Grammar, a song book, the Keepsake Annual for 1836, and a certain book with 10 plates, published by the Plaintiff in the year of our Lord 1827, and purporting to be published by John Joseph Stockdale in the year of our Lord 1827, which said last-mentioned book is the book mentioned in the Declaration as the book mentioned to be a book of a most disgusting nature in the said book published by the Defendants, as in the Declaration mentioned, purporting to be Reports of the Inspectors of Prisons of Great Britain; and the Defendants aver that the said book so found and so mentioned to be of a most disgusting nature as aforesaid, to wit, when it was so found as aforesaid, to wit, on the said 1st day of March A. D. 1836, contained 10 plates and divers, to wit, 300 pages of printed letters, words and figures; and that the said last-mentioned book then and always thereafter was and is of a most disgusting nature, and that the plates thereof and each and every of them, to wit, then and always thereafter were and are obscene and indecent in the extreme; and the Defendants aver that before the said last-mentioned book was so found in the said gaol as aforesaid, and before the publishing of the said alleged libel, to wit, on the 1st day of May in the year of our Lord 1827, the said last-mentioned book was and had been published by the said Plaintiff as such bookseller and publisher, as in the Declaration mentioned, and in his said trade and business; and that the Plaintiff, as such bookseller and publisher as aforesaid, was the publisher as in the said Reports and alleged libel mentioned of the said last-mentioned book, being the book so found as aforesaid, and in respect of the mention whereof in the said alleged libel the Plaintiff hath complained as aforesaid in his said Declaration; and the said William Crawford and Whitworth Russell did afterwards, to wit, on the 1st day of March in the year of our Lord 1836 make their separate and distinct report in writing of the state of the said gaol, and then transmitted the same to the Right Hon. John Russell, Esq., (commonly called the Right Hon. Lord John Russell), Esq.

then

Appendix, No. 2.

Stockdale v. Hansard.

Plea.

then being one of His Majesty's Principal Secretaries of State, which said Report, amongst other things, contained the words, matters and things complained of in the said Declaration; and the Defendants aver that by the word "We" being the first of the said words of the said alleged libel so complained of in the said Declaration, and being contained in the said Report, it was intended to signify, and that the said word "We" in the alleged libel and Report did and does signify and purport to signify the said William Crawford and Whitworth Russell, and afterwards, to wit, on the day and year last aforesaid the Defendants printed and published divers, to wit, 200 copies of the said Report so transmitted to the said Secretary of State as aforesaid, which said copies and each of them so by them the Defendants printed and published, contained, amongst other things, the words, matters and things in the said Declaration complained of as they lawfully might for the cause aforesaid, which said last-mentioned printing and publishing is the same publishing and causing to be published as in the said Declaration mentioned and therein complained of; and this they the Defendants are ready to verify, &c.

Charles Crompton.

---

1. The General Issue.
2. That the words complained of in the Declaration are true.

In the King's Bench, Tuesday the 22d day of November, 1836, in the 7th year of King William the Fourth.

Stockdale v. Hansard & Others. } Upon reading the Order of the Hon. Mr. Justice Littledale, dated this day, it is ordered that the Defendants have leave to plead several matters, (to wit); that they are not guilty; and for further Plea, that the words complained of in the Declaration are true.

Parkes & P.

By the Court.

Stockdale v. Hansard & Others.—Replication.

In the King's Bench, the 16th day of December, in the year of our Lord 1836.

Replication.

Stockdale v. Hansard & Others. } And the said Plaintiff, as to the Plea of the said Defendants by them first above pleaded, whereof they have put themselves upon the country, doth the like. And as to the said Plea of the said Defendants by them secondly above pleaded, the said Plaintiff says that the said book, with 10 plates, in the said last-mentioned Plea and in the said Declaration mentioned as being published by the said Plaintiff in the year 1827, is not of a most disgusting nature, and the said plates in the said book are not, nor is either of them in any manner obscene and indecent, as in and by the said last-mentioned Plea is averred, and this the said Plaintiff prays may be inquired of by the country.

J. Curwood.

King's Bench.—*Stockdale v. Hansard & Others.*

Monday the 9th day of January to rejoin.

Entered,

To Messrs. Parkes & Preston, Defendants' Attornies.

Yours, &c.

T. B. Howard, Plaintiff's Attorney.

4 January 1837.

Hansard & Others at the suit of Stockdale.—Rejoinder.

In the King's Bench, the 6th day of January, in the year of our Lord 1837.

Rejoinder.

Hansard & Others, *at the suit of* Stockdale. } And the said Defendants, as to the Replication of the said Plaintiff to the said Plea of the said Defendants by them secondly above pleaded, and which the said Plaintiff prays may be inquired of by the country, do the like.

Charles Crompton.

Appendix, No. 3.

Appendix, No. 3.

STATEMENTS by Messrs. *Hansard* respecting the

PUBLICATION, CIRCULATION and SALE of VOTES, REPORTS and PAPERS Printed by Order of THE HOUSE, prior to and since the Order for the Sale of such Papers, 1641-1836.

LIST OF PAPERS.

I.—STATEMENT of the Practice of the Printing, Publishing and Sale of the VOTES and PARLIAMENTARY PAPERS, from the earliest period of record, 1641 to 1777.

Many of the particulars mentioned in the following Statement, are taken from the Papers as originally printed, and which are preserved in the collections in the British Museum, and in the Library of the House of Commons. The Journals are referred to, when any entry occurs in them directing the mode of publication.

The earliest description of Printing sanctioned by Parliament was the Votes and Proceedings of the House.

1641. Among the tracts in the old library of the British Museum, forming part of the collection called the King's Pamphlets, are several printed papers, Resolutions, Addresses and Orders, drawn out in the Parliamentary form—thus:

See Collection of the King's Pamphlets in the B. M. vol. i. p. 12. 27.

Die Veneris, 30° Julii 1641.

Resolution on questions, &c., and so on, recording these Resolutions, that the protestation made by the House of Commons for defending the Protestant religion, and the power and privilege of Parliament, is proper to be taken; and ordering the Members to send down copies to the places which they represent; the last resolution being, "That these Votes shall be printed and attested under the clerk's hand." This is the earliest printed paper that the present search can discover with the denomination of "Votes."

This is the first mention in the Journals of *Votes* and Proceedings of The House.

Journals, vol. ii. 230.

In the collections of printed papers in the British Museum, and in the Library of the House of Commons, are several Declarations, Remonstrances, Resolutions and Orders of the House in 1641, mostly having the order to be published as well as printed.

King's Pamphlets, vol. i. p. 39. 47. 48. 59. 198. B. M. collection, vol. 11. 27, 28, 29.

1641. Declarations respecting the illegality of proceedings against the five Members, are ordered "to be drawn up in one declaration, to the end that it may be forthwith *published in print*."

Journals, vol. ii. p. 374.

1641. "Ordered, That the printer shall be required forthwith to print a sufficient number of the Protestations and Declarations touching the late breach of privilege; and the knights, burgesses, &c. are to send them down to their several counties, cities and boroughs respectively, with all speed."

Journals, vol. ii. p. 389.

1641. The three Declarations, drawn into one form, "Resolved, That the Declaration be forthwith *published in print*."

Journals, vol. ii. p. 383.

In 1642, a Committee was appointed "to consider of the means of divulging, dispersing and publishing the Orders and Votes, and the well and true printing of them." This became a Standing Committee, and matters relating to printing were referred to it. On a Report made to The House of the manner of transmitting the Votes in packages to the headboroughs, tithingmen, &c., The House resolved that particular papers should be printed, and specified the number of copies of each, varying from 4,000 to 9,000.

Journals, vol. ii. p. 604. 609. 616.

The collection in the British Museum has many copies, showing what these Votes consisted of, mixed up with a great variety of the political tracts of that period. In one of the volumes of this collection are several Orders of The House and Ordinances. One is an order to the sheriffs, which is ordered to be printed and *published*; and is signed by the clerk, *H. Elsinge*. Another is headed, "*The Votes of the Parliament*, 19 *May* 1642;" and are resolutions against arresting Lords and Members of the House, and resolving to maintain them in what they have done in obedience to their commands. Another is headed, "*Votes, die Martis, Julii* 1642," and then sets forth five Resolutions. On the 12th of July is an Order respecting Volunteers; and on the 28th is a Declaration for protecting those employed by

See Collection of the King's Pamphlets, B. M. vol. 6, passim.
Ibid. vol. ii. p. 33.
Ibid. p. 111.
Ibid. p. 119. 120.

Ibid. p. 15. 20. 62. 73. 74. 77. 116. 139. 152. 158. 160. 213. 240. Ibid. p. 100, 103.

by the House. All these are signed by the clerk, with an order to be printed forthwith. They with many others have the imprint of Husbands, which states that they are *sold* at his shop. There are likewise several orders of committees signed in MS.

Journals, vol. ii. p. 583.

1642. "Ordered, That it be referred to a Committee to prepare the letter and instruction for the Committee at York, to prepare an Order for the knights and burgesses, to take care of the *publishing*, in the several counties of the kingdom, *the Orders and Declarations of both Houses.*"

King's Pamphlets, B. M. vol. 3. p. 54.

In 1642 there is an Order against Members wilfully neglecting the service of the House, for which their estates are to be sequestered. This is ordered to be printed forthwith, and is signed by *H. Elsinge*, Cler. Parl. D. Com. The imprint is by Husbands, *and is sold* at his shop, Middle Temple.

Ibid. vol. 3°. p. 91.

In the same year is "Prince Rupert's Cruell Warrant," ordering the sending in provisions to the troops lying at Tocester, "at your utmost perills, as total plundering and burning of your houses and what other mischiefs the licenced and hungry souldier can inflict upon you:" which is ordered by the House of Commons to be *forthwith printed and set up on posts.*

Ibid.

There are several Ordinances, printed on broad sheets, and some Orders on small leaves, and attested in the same form, with the imprint to them; but the notification of sale is not always affixed.

Ibid. 54, 55, 58.

In another series of the collection is a Letter from Lord Fairfax, together with "a relation of all the passages at the great meeting at York," signed by H. Elsinge, Cler. Parl. D. Com. Printed *and sold* by A. Norton for John Franke, Fleet-street.

There are several other papers with the official order for printing, but without the notification of sale; and some have the expression, to be printed *and published.*

Ibid.

The Committee for Printing ordered a book to be printed, called "Good Courage discovered and encouraged, by Simeon Ash, preacher in London," which is notified *as sold* at the Golden Dragon, Fleet-street. A similar notification is affixed to a relation of occurrences in Donegal, Londonderry, Tyrone, and Fermanagh.

Ibid. vol. v. p. 99. 431; and S. C. Collection of Parl. Papers in H. C. Library, vols. 62. 63.

Resuming the search in the Museum, it will be found to contain many Votes of 1647–48, on various sized paper, chiefly single leaves, like placards; and some are headed with the title, "Votes." These are expressed as printed and published by Edward Husbands, printer to the Hon. House of Commons. Some have the title of Ordinances. One is the Declaration of Parliament, ordered on the 6th of June 1647 to be printed *and published.* Others are Votes, Orders and Resolutions, on the 18th of March and 2d to 12th of June. Two are entitled, "Several Votes of the Commons, assembled in Parliament," and contain Orders in the form they are now drawn up in the Proceedings in Parliament, and printed on a broad sheet. They are ordered to be printed *and published,* and signed by H. Elsinge, Cler. Parl. D. Com. Besides the usual order and licence for printing subjoined to these, the purpose of *publishing* is expressly mentioned, but to what extent they were sold does not appear.

King's Pamphlets, vol. ii. p. 213. vol. iv. p. 19. vol. v. p. 21.

The publishing was effected in various other ways than by *sale*; some were ordered to be read in all churches and chapels; some by being published by the common cryer on the Exchange; and others by beat of drum and sound of trumpet. The extensive dispersion of many of these Votes must in a great part, if not wholly, have been gratuitous, although the imprint, in the usual form of a bookseller's notification, makes it probable that the sale of them was one means of dispersion. It is evident that during the time of the Commonwealth the printing must have been very considerable, and that it was intended for dispersion and general knowledge.

Journals, vol. viii. pp. 6. 14. 15. 17. 18. 19. 25. 45. 53. 58. 70. 74. 80. 103. 134. 149. 307; and S. C. Collection, vol. 76. 78; and King's Pamphlets, vol. 18.

In 1660, the several proceedings for the Restoration of the King, and the Declarations and Resolutions of the House connected with that event, are expressly ordered to be *printed and published*; and in 1660 and 1661 the authenticity of the printing by appointment and licence of the Speaker, is frequently enforced by the Orders of the House.

1660. King Charles' letter to the Speaker, and letter to General Monk, and His Majesty's Declaration, are ordered to be forthwith *printed and published.*

Declaration of the House for putting off Easter Term; ordered to be forthwith *printed and published.*

Declaration for continuing the Sheriffs, ordered to be *printed and published.*

Votes and Orders for His Majesty's speedy return to Parliament; and for restoring the King's Arms; ordered to be forthwith *printed and published.*

Ordered, That the letter sent to His Majesty from this House, in answer to His Majesty's letter to this House, *be forthwith printed and published.*

Ordered, That the Declaration for bringing in the duty of Excise, and the arrear thereof, be forthwith *printed and published.*

Ordered, That the Ordinance for three months' assessment be forthwith *published.*

Ordered, That the Act for putting in execution the powers of the Ordinance, be forthwith "*printed and published for the use of the Members* of this House."

Message from the King for an Act of Pardon and Oblivion, ordered to be forthwith *printed and published.*

The

The preceding particulars are extracted from the entries in the Journals. The corresponding ones are likewise expressed on the copies of the printed papers in the British Museum, and the collection in the Library of the House of Commons. Appendix, No. 3.

1660. "A Declaration of the Lords and Commons for suppressing tumults;" ordered to be *forthwith printed and published*. King's Pamphlets, vol. 18, p. 7.

A Proclamation declaring his Majesty's right to the throne, and professing the loyalty of Parliament, concluding with "God save the King." May 8, ordered to be *forthwith printed and published*. Ibid. p. 10, 11.

A Declaration of the Commons of the state of progress of the Act for securing the Protestant religion; ordered to be *forthwith printed and published*. Ibid. p. 12.

Order for all ministers to pray for the King; to return thanks for his gracious letters; and enjoining them to be read in all churches and chapels. 9 May, ordered to be *forthwith printed and published*. Ibid. p. 14.

Order for taking down the Arms of the Commonwealth, and for setting up the King's Arms instead thereof. 9 May, ordered to be *forthwith printed and published*. Ibid. p. 15.

Ordered, that Commissioners of Admiralty, of Excise and other Officers, do continue in the exercise of their authority. May 11, ordered to be *forthwith printed and published*. Ibid. p. 19.

There are several other orders and declarations at this period, with the same order for *printing and publishing*. They are signed by Wm. Jessop, clerk of the Commons' House of Parliament. Ibid.

Ordered, That the Act of Tonnage and Poundage, and the Book of Rates, together with the Rules annexed, be forthwith *printed and published*. S. G. Collection, vol. vi.

Ordered, That the Act for continuing the Excise "be printed by the printer of this House according to the original remaining in this House." Journals, vol. viii. p. 105. Ibid. p. 189.

Resolved, That "the Summary Reasons against the Bill for Reforming and Governing the Corporations, by Mr. Pryn, a Member, is an illegal, false, scandalous and seditious pamphlet;" and upon his submission, Resolved, "That the House is satisfied;" "and Ordered, That these Votes and Resolutions be forthwith *printed and published*." Ibid. p. 302.

1662. The Votes for delivering certain ecclesiastical records to the Archbishop of Canterbury, are "Ordered to be printed and published, that all persons concerned may take notice thereof." Journals, vol. viii. p. 418.

In 1679, the Journals has an entry of a resolution against the validity of Earl Danby's pardon, and the vote containing it is *ordered* to be posted up at Westminster Hall gate. From the placard-form of printing the Votes, this was easily to be done. A similar mode of publication was directed in 1728, against Members' protections. Journals, vol. ix. p. 612. vol. xxiii. p. 205.

The Library of the House of Commons contains one volume of "Votes and Proceedings of the two last Parliaments in 1680 and 1681, the first holden at Westminster and the last at Oxford." The order for printing, which is the first generally made, was on the 30th October. (Journals, vol. ix. p. 642.) These votes take the shape of foolscap folio, and which they have preserved to the present time. Given to the Library by the Rt. Hon. C. W. W. Wynn, M.P., and saved from the fire which destroyed the two Houses.

In No. 7 of these, it is ordered that the Informations of the Popish Plot be printed; and *that Dangerfield should have the benefit of the Printing*. Of course by *the sale* of the copies, because two other persons are licensed as the Printers, who must have been paid for the labour with profit for that part of the business. In the library of the House of Commons is a copy of the Informations of Dangerfield, Bedlow, Dugdale and others: they all have the Speaker's authority to be printed, with the bookseller's imprint in the title-page. 1680. Nov. 9, and Journals, vol. ix. p. 649. S. G. Collection, vol. 78.

In Nos. 13, 16 and 38, *Notifications* are inserted, by way of advertisement, that the Informations are printed and *published* according to the order of the House, by the appointment and licence of the Speaker, and stating that they may be had at the printing house. 1680. Nov. 16. Nov. 19. 1681. Jan. 10.

On the 20th November there is an entry in the Journals, that the letters and papers relating to the plot be printed, and Mr. Treby to take care thereof. In vol. 82 of the collection of Tracts and Papers in the House of Commons' library, are the original printed copies of these papers, with the authority for printing signed by Mr. Treby (as deputed by the House), and with the bookseller's imprint. Journals, vol. ix. p. 658. S. G. Collection, vol. 82.

In Nos. 40 and 50 the appointment to print is to Gabriel Kunholt; and the imprint is, "Printed by Thomas Snowden, bookseller to Prince Rupert, *and sold* at his shop at the King's Head, over against the House." Votes, 1680. 13.

No. 2, Oxford. The Votes have the notification of sale. Votes, 1680-1. Mar. 24.

No. 4. This Vote contains an order for printing the examinations relative to the plot, and has the notification of the paper being *sold* at Kunholt's shop. Ib. Mar. 25.

The speeches of Sir William Williams, as Speaker of the House, at Oxford, on the 21st March 1680, were *sold* at Kunholt's shop. The Speaker's authority is printed at the back of the title, stating the necessity of correcting the falsehoods of unlicensed copies. And at the Votes, 1680, and S. G. Collection, vol. 89.

Appendix, No 3.

the end of Votes No. 4, is a "☞ Whereas in consequence of the imperfect printing of the speeches, a correct edition, by the *Speaker's own order and authority*, is printed and sold by Kembolt."

Votes, 1680, and Journals, vol. ix. p. 69.

The Resolutions and Reports relating to the impeachment of Sir W. Scroggs and others, have the imprint of J. Wright, &c. at the Crown, Ludgate-hill, and at the Rose and Crown, St. Paul's Church-yard; and the Report, Examinations and Resolutions for the impeachment of Richard Thompson, has the appointment and imprint of Francis Smith and Benjamin Harris.

The Examinations relative to the plot, and the Reports on the impeachments, are of the nature of what would at this day be deemed Parliamentary Papers. Some are noticed as being *for sale*, others have the bookseller's imprint, and in all probability were sold in the same way.

See Collection in the B. M. Journals, vol. x. pp. 12. 43. 273. 281. 352. 454.

1689. The votes in the volume of this year have the usual appointment of a printer, and the bookseller's imprint; but they have no express notice of sale. The scantiness of information at this period may be accounted for by the unsettled practice of the House; for in 1689 two motions for printing the Votes were negatived. In 1689 to 1695, they were ordered to be printed; and the form of entry is the same as that now used in the Journals for appointing the printing and giving authority to the publication.

Lords' Jour. vol. xv. p. 72.

31 December 1691 and 2 January 1691–2. The Lords came to a resolution "that the printed Vote of the House of Commons is sufficient ground for the Lords to take notice of that Vote to the House of Commons."

Upon which Mr. Hatsell remarks,

Hatsell, vol. ii. p. 37, 34.

"Indeed the practice that has so long prevailed, of printing the Votes, may have rendered such a proceeding unnecessary (searching the Commons' Journals by the Lords). It has however happened that this practice has been interrupted. On the 26th of February 1702, it is resolved, 'That it be a standing order of The House, That no Votes of the House shall be printed without the particular Order of The House;' and the order for printing that had been made at the beginning of that session, is discharged; and the reason for this proceeding is mentioned in the Journal, 'That the House have found great inconveniencies attending the printing of the Votes.' [The Lords' interference as an Address by the Commons to the Queen.] But this restriction did not last long; at the beginning of the next session this matter was again debated; and on the 22d of November 1702 it was carried, on a division, 177 to 147, 'That the Votes should be printed;' and so, I believe, it has continued every session since that time. Indeed, nothing seems more unreasonable, I might say unjust, than that the *proceedings* (I do not say the *debates*) of the House of Commons should not, by some means or other, and that with authority, be conveyed to their constituents; more especially since private bills, so generally affecting the interests both of the landed and commercial proprietors, have become so numerous." The same writer says,

Com. Jour. xiv. p. 231.

Hatsell, vol. ii. p. 118.

"On the 29 Jan. 1705, the Speaker, in justification of the manner of making a particular entry on the Votes, states that the rule of entering is founded in great prudence and good sense; as there may be many questions proposed which it may be imprudent to *publish to the world*."

Collection of Votes, in B. M.

From 1690 to 1711, the notice *of sale* is expressed, and on a considerable number of the Votes the price of 1 *d.*, 2 *d.* and 4 *d.* is printed. The price of 2 *d.* is most general.

In 1711, the Report of the Committee on Public Accounts was printed, under the same appointment as the Votes, and with the same bookseller's imprint, and the *price* of 6 *d.* is affixed to it; and the *price* of 2 *d.* is printed on a Representation to the Queen. The Speaker's congratulatory Address to Mr. Harley, on his escape from the attempted assassination by De Guiscard, was ordered to be printed, and *sold*, having the price of 2 *d.* printed on it.

An Address to the Queen was printed in this year; which is stated as *sold for* 1 *d.*

In 1712, the Treaty with the States-General; and in 1714, the Army Half-pay List were printed under the same appointment as the Votes; and have the same bookseller's imprint to them, but no notice of sale but what may be inferred from the bookseller's imprint. But in 1715, the Report on Poor and Scavenger Rates was printed, and has *the price of* 4 *d.* affixed to it. One edition has no price printed on it.

The Votes in 1715 and 1716 have the *price of* 2 *d.* affixed to them.

From 1717 to 1721, the appointment and licence to print is in the usual form, but no express mention of the sale. They have the bookseller's imprint in the usual way.

In 1717, the Report of the Commission of Inquiry into Recusants' Estates was ordered to be printed.

In 1718, the Report of Debts due to Scotland.

In 1719, another Report on Recusants' Estates.

In 1720, an Address to the King was printed; and a Report on Subscriptions for Fisheries, Insurance, Annuities, &c.

Most of these have the appointment and licence for printing in the same form, and signed by the Speaker. In some instances the Order for printing is entered on the back of the title, and signed by the Chief Clerk, but they have not the Speaker's appointment. No price is affixed, and the notice of sale is the bookseller's imprint.

In

In 1722 the appointment is to Jacob Tonson, Bernard Lintot, and William Taylor, and the same names are in the bookseller's imprint, with the places of residence and signs of their shops. It is well known that these persons were booksellers, not in partnership, and carrying on independent trade, but associated together in a joint venture in printing this or other books, according to a practice peculiar to the bookselling trade. The printing was done by some printer who was paid for his labour, and the profits of sale divided between the appointees. Appendix, No. 8.

In 1721 several Reports were printed; some of the original editions are in the British Museum collection. Some are reprinted in the collection of the 15 volumes of the House of Commons' Reports, 1803; as the Reports on Scotch Forfeited Estates, in 1719 to 1725. Others are not reprinted in those volumes, but are bound up in the collection in the British Museum: as the Report on Popish Recusants in 1720; and the Reports from the Trustees of the Estates of the Directors of the South Sea Company, in 1722 and 1723. All these have the same appointment and licence for printing as is subjoined to the Votes, and have the same form of bookseller's imprint. Instead of the words now used of "Ordered, by The House of Commons, to be printed," the words used are "*Published by order of the House of Commons.*" These, with all similar Reports mentioned in this statement, are printed in the same form, and are bound up with the daily Votes.

From 1738 to 1729 the same form of order continues in the Votes, with the same kind of bookseller's imprint.

From 1751 the Votes assume a settled form, and after 1748 the proceedings are entered more in detail, and the petitions begin to be entered in full; and which practice continued till the alterations in the form took place in 1817. At that time their bulk, on account of the increased number of petitions, had become inconvenient. The abstracted form now in use was adopted, and such petitions as are specially ordered, are printed in an appendix. The appointment and licence to print is uniformly the same, and the bookseller's imprint in the usual terms. From 1721 notices are sometimes entered at the end of the year's Votes, stating that "complete sets may be had." But the word *sold* occurs in 1770, and continues on the daily Vote till 1803. The Speaker's appointment from that time is entered at the beginning of the session; the bookseller's imprint was discontinued, but the sale was made known by separate notices and advertisements.

Any further examination of the Votes subsequent to 1729 was unnecessary for the purpose of ascertaining from them any additional circumstances relating to the publication and sale, as Mr. Nichols, in his examination before the Committee on Printing in 1822, brings down the practice of sale from that period to the present time. He says that "from the year 1729 to 1777 the Votes were printed by J. Nichols, senior, and his predecessor, Mr. Bowyer; and that they, after deducting the expenses, accounted to The Speaker for the profit, which, from 1768 to 1778, amounted on an average to about 240 *l.* a year." "From 1778 the sale gradually diminished (occasioned by the proceedings of The House being regularly detailed in the newspapers), till, in 1777, there was an actual loss, when the then Speaker, Sir Fletcher Norton, transferred the account to the Treasury." "About 200 copies each day are now sold." Rep. 1822 (607) p. 120. In 1822.

In 1768, an order of the House requiring the magistrates of Middlesex to preserve the peace at Brentford during an election, and assuring the sheriffs of the support and protection of the House, was ordered to be printed and published. Journals, vol. xxxii. p. 90.

In 1729 to 1731 several Reports and Papers were printed with the usual orders and imprints. A List of Annuities, printed in 1780, has the *price* 6*s.* affixed to it.

In 1781 and 1785 the Reports on the List of Officers and Fees of the Courts of Westminster-hall; on the Derwentwater Estates; on the Charitable Corporation; on the Cottonian Library; and on the York Buildings Water Company—were printed. All of these have the Speaker's appointment of the printing, with the bookseller's imprint: the Report on the Charitable Corporation, and on the Cottonian Library, has, printed on the last leaf of each of them, the *price* of 6 *d.*; and the List of Officers and Fees has the *price of* 6 *d.* printed on the title-page.

The Reports printed in 1748 and those of several following years, have the words in the title-page, "Printed in the year 1748," &c., but no bookseller's imprint. A Report in 1771 has the words "*Published* by Order of the House of Commons," together with the bookseller's imprint, as in cases where printed for sale. In 1777 the words "Ordered to be printed," occur without any bookseller's notification of sale; and this form of words is generally used to 1800, when the present words, "Ordered, by The House of Commons, to be printed," were adopted. See the collection of early reports, 1744 to 1800, as originally printed, H. C. library, vol. i. to xxviii. and from 1801 to the present time, passim.

Appendix, No. 3.

Journals, vol. xxi. p. 848. 895. 897. 799. xxii. p. 13. xxiv. 783. 837. xxv. 773. 780. xxvi. 430. 493. xxix. 845. 1010. xxxiv. 383. 706.

In 1731 to 1773 the form of order for printing, as entered in the Journals, is, "that a sufficient number of copies be printed for the use of the Members of the House." But there are frequent variations in the same years; in many instances in the same year the usual entry is made, "with the appointment and injunction against presuming to print without authority," and in some cases the abbreviated order is used, "that this Report be printed."

(¹) Journals, xxxv. 198. 315. 801. xxxvi. 998. xxxvii. 1036; xxxviii. 411. 450. 863; and xxxix. to lvii. passim.

From 1774 to 1802 the words "sufficient for the use of the Members of the House"¹ is almost invariably used. But from 1802 to 1807 the phrase is abridged to "printed for the Members of the House."² After that year the words used are, "that the Report be printed;"³ and in 1817, when the Report "on the method of preparing the Votes" was made, the same form of entry was confirmed, and continues in use at this time.

(²) lviii. 40. 124. 288. 308 and lix. to lxi. passim. (³) lxii to xci. passim.

Journals, vol. xxi. 848. 813. 807. 870. 910. xxii. 13. 149. 169. 172. 481. 483. Journals, xxi. 894. 896.

The Reports on the Derwentwater Estate in 1731, on the Charitable Corporation and on the Cottonian Library in 1732, on the York Buildings Company in 1733, mentioned above, have in the Journals the order for printing "sufficient copies for the use of Members," and have likewise on the printed copies the bookseller's imprint. But the List of Fees in 1732 has the appointment to print with the injunction against unlicensed printing in the Journals, with the *price of sale affixed* to the printed copy; and the Reports on the Charitable Corporation, and on the Cottonian Library, have likewise the *price* affixed to them. The Report on the Charitable Corporation was first ordered as above mentioned, and a few days afterwards with the Speaker's appointment. In 1771 the case occurs of the Report on Obstructions to the Orders of the House, which has the words "*published* by order of the House," with the bookseller's imprint on the printed copies; and the order in the Journals has the appointment to print with the usual injunction. This is the last occurrence of that kind having any indication of sale.

Journals, xxxiii. 362.

The particulars mentioned in Statement H. subjoined, show some instances out of many of the number of copies remaining after supplying *the use of Members* and others, during the periods from 1731 to 1807, when that expression was used, and from 1807 to 1835, when *ordered to be printed* only was expressed, and during which period a very extensive gratuitous circulation has taken place, up to the time of the authorized Sale commencing in 1836.

Journals, vol. xxiv. 213. 682.

Journals, vol. xxxi. p. 419. xxxiv. p. 383.

The Journals were first printed in 1742, and from the proposals of Mr. Hardinge, the chief clerk, it may be supposed the Members were familiarized to the purchase of the copies of their Proceedings and Reports. He proposed that the expense of printing the Journals should be defrayed by subscriptions at a certain price per copy. In 1767 and 1773, the collection of Reports in large folio was first made, being a reprint of such as were not inserted in the Journals. It may be supposed that the Reports now became too voluminous and expensive to be an object of private speculation of profit by sale. The printing of the Votes had taken a settled form and practice, the sale being uniformly continued, though, in time, ceasing to defray the expense, and to be a profitable undertaking, however convenient to the community. Some effect of this kind might have been produced on the practice of selling Parliamentary Reports and Papers, both by the printing the Journals and reprinting the Reports.

The present House of Commons' Printing establishment dates its commencement in 1782; from which time the practice of gratuitous circulation of Parliamentary Papers to Members, and by The Speaker's orders, has generally prevailed, with occasional exceptions, till the re-establishment of the Sale by the Resolution of The House in August 1835.

Extracts from the S. G. Collection of Parl. Papers in the H. C. Library.

STATEMENT of Particulars derived from an Inspection of the Collection of Ancient Parliamentary Papers and Tracts in the Library of the House of Commons, formerly in the Speaker's Gallery; showing the mode of Ordering the Printing and Publishing. From 1640 to 1709.

1640. Appointment of a Committee to receive Petitions against Ministers. Vol. 22.	This wants the usual order for printing, to authenticate its official character.
1641. Declaration of the Commons, 9 September. Vol 21.	Ordered to be *printed and published*.
1641. Remonstrance of the House of Commons on the State of the Kingdom; 15 December 1641. Vol. 21.	Order for printing. (signed) *H. Elsinge*, Cler. Parl. D. Com.

Appendix, No. 3.

Extracts from the S. C. Collection of Parl. Papers in the H. C. Library.

1641. Declaration of Lords and Commons, with additional Reasons; 12 March. Vol. 21.	Ordered to be printed and *published.* (signed) *John Brown*, Cler. Parl. *H. Elsynge*, Cler. Parl. D. Com.
1640–42. Impeachments of Strafford and Laud; and several other papers. Vol. 27.	Stated as printed and *published* by order of the House of Commons; but *qu.* if these are the original printed copies, or reprinted as pamphlet publications?
1641–42. The order of the House of Commons and Declaration of the Breach of Privilege by His Majesty coming in person with armed men to the House of Commons. And the power given to the Committee of the House of Commons to sit in London to consider of vindicating the Privilege of Parliament. Meeting in Guildhall; *Master Wilde, Serjeant-at-Law*, sitting in the chair of that Committee; 6 Jan 1642. Vol. 28.	Signed by *H. Elsynge*, Cler. Parl. D. Com. 9 Jan. 1642. With the bookseller's imprint.
1642. Petition of the Lords and Commons against the King's journey to Ireland; 18 April 1642. Vol. 28.	Ordered to be *published* in print. (signed) *H. Elsynge*, Cler. Parl. D. Com.
Several Remonstrances and Declarations.	Signed in the same manner.
1642. Letters from Lord Digby. Vol. 61.	Ordered to be *published in print.* (signed) *H. Elsynge*, Cler. Parl. D. Com.
1642. Declaration of Parliament for raising the Trained-bands; 9 Aug. Vol. 66.	Ordered to be *forthwith printed and published.* (signed) *H. Elsynge*, Cler. Parl. D. Com.
1642. Declaration concerning his Majesty's Proclamation; 19 Aug. Vol. 59.	Same order and signing; with the booksellers' imprint, as sold at their shops.
1642. His Majesty's Message concerning an Order of the House for borrowing Money; 6 Sep. Vol. 62.	Ordered by the Commons to be *forthwith printed and published.* (signed) *H. Elsynge*, Cler. Parl. D. Com. and *sold* at the bookseller's shop.
1642. Message from the King to the Lords and Commons; 6 Sep. Vol. 62.	Signed by *J. Brown*, Cler. Parl. *H. Elsynge*, Cler. Parl. Dom. Com.
1642. Letter to Mr. Pym from the Earl of Essex, relating to the spreading of false intelligence. Vol. 62.	Ordered by the House of Commons to be *forthwith printed and published.* *H. Elsynge*, Cler. Parl. D. Com. Printed by L. N. for Husbands, and sold by him.
1642. Propositions for raising horse; 19 Sep. Vol. 62.	Ordered to be printed and sent into the several counties, cities, &c. (signed) *H. Elsynge*, Cler. Parl. D. Com. Husbands, printer, and sold at his shop.
1642. Declaration of the Lords and Commons, in Answer to the Scots' Declaration; 23 Sep. Vol. 62.	Ordered by the Lords and Commons to be forthwith *printed and published.* (signed) *H. Elsynge*, Cler. Parl. D. Com. Printed and *sold* by Husbands.
1642. Petition of the Lords and Commons, to be sent to the King by the Earl of Essex; Sep. Vol. 62.	Similar order; and notice to be *sold.*
1642. Declaration and Protestation of the Lords and Commons; 22 Oct. Vol. 62.	Ordered to be printed and published, and read in all churches and chapels.
1642. Declaration of the Lords and Commons in favour of persons advancing money on the credit of the late Ordinance; 29 Nov. Vol. 62.	Ordered to be forthwith *printed and published.* Signed by *J. Brown*, Cler. Parl. At the end is an "Order of the Commons' House of Parliament for enforcing the restitution of goods unlawfully seized," which is signed by *H. Elsynge*, Cler. Parl. D. Com.

Appendix, No. 3.

Extracts from the S. O. Collection of Parl. Papers in the H. C. Library.

1643. The Solemn League and Covenant; 25 Sep. Vol. 69.

Ordered to be *printed and published*.
H. Elsynge, Cler. Parl. D. Com.

The Votes, Orders, Resolutions, Remonstrances and Ordinances of Parliament, from 1641 to 1646, were collected together and reprinted by Husbands, by direction of the House, and arranged chronologically, and printed with continuous paging. They form two volumes; to each of which is prefixed an Index. The mode *of ordering the printing and publication* is repeated at the close of each paper.

Volume 1.

1641 to 1642. An exact collection of all Remonstrances, Declarations, Votes, Ordinances, &c. From 1641 to 1643 [qy. 1642.]

In the H. C. Library.

Printed by Edward Husbands, and *sold* by him, 1642.

At the back of the last page is an order for printing, and "that Edward Husbands, stationer, shall have the benefit of printing the book, and that no person do presume to print the same without the said Master Husbands' consent, during the space of six months."

H. Elsynge, Cler. Dom. Com.

Volume 2.

1642 to 1646. A collection of all public Ordinances and Declarations of both Houses of Parliament, from March 1642 to 1646.

In the H. C. Library.

Aug. 6, 1644. "Ordered, That Mr. Husbands, the printer, do print all the Orders, &c., that have passed since the setting forth of the last volume, formerly set forth by him; and that no other person do presume to print the same." He is likewise enjoined to "take care diligently to compare the coppies with the originals." *H. Elsynge*, C. Dom. Com.

Printed by T. W. for E. Husbands, printer to the Hon. House of Commons, and *sold* at his shop. 1646.

[*From this time to 1680 many Parliamentary Documents of a similar kind are to be found in this collection, which are not here noticed.*]

1660. The King's letter to the Speaker, with His Majesty's Declaration; and General Monck's letter; 1 May. Vol. 75.

Resolution of the House, That they be *forthwith printed and published*.
(signed) *Wm. Jessop*, Clerk of the Commons' House of Parliament.

1660. The King's Message, 16 June. Vol. 78.

Same order and signing; 20 June.

1660. Book of Rates of Tonnage and Poundage, and Rules. Vol. 6.

Ordered to be forthwith printed *and published*.

1680. Examinations of Bedlow, and Dangerfield's, Dugdale's and others Informations relating to the Popish Plot. Vol 78.

Order to print and appointment of printer.
Signed by *W. Williams*, Speaker.
With the bookseller's imprint.

1680. King's Message and Address thereon relating to Tangier.

Impeachment of Sir W. Scroggs, of Richard Thompson, and several informations relating to the Plot. Vol. 82.

Similar order and appointment.

1680. Letters and Papers relating to the Plot, committed to the care of Mr. Treby, chairman of the Committee of Secrecy. Vol. 82.

Order to print and appointment of printer.
Signed by Mr. *Treby*, in pursuance of the order of the House.

1680. Informations of Sergeant and Maurice relating to the Impeachments. Vol. 82.

Order to print and appointment of printer.
Signed by *W. Williams*, Speaker.
With notification in the bookseller's imprint as *sold* at Kunholt's shop.

1688. Declaration of Rights; 12 Feb. Vol. 80.

Ordered to be *printed and published*; 13 Feb.

Appendix No. 3.

Extracts from the S. G. Collection of Parl. Papers in the H. C. Library.

1701. State of proceedings on the Impeached Lords. Vol. 81.	Order for printing. Signed by *Paul Jodrell*, Cl' Dom' Com'. At the end is "By virtue of an Order of the House of Commons;" then follows the appointment of the printer, signed "*Ro. Harley*, Speaker."
1702. Bill against Occasional Conformity. Vol. 81.	Ordered by the House of Commons to be printed.
1702. Report on the Conference with the Lords on the proceedings respecting the Commissioners of Accounts. Vol. 81.	*Published* by order of the House of Commons; and at the end is the appointment of the printer, signed *Ro. Harley*, Speaker.

From the preceding statement it appears,—

1. That the first appearance of the printed Votes of the House of Commons, though in a very incipient state, was in 1641.

2. That in 1642 to 1649, or so much of that period as afforded any examples, they became numerous, and all in the form of placards; a great proportion, however, being called Orders and Ordinances.

3. That in 1680 they assumed a settled uniform shape, which has continued uninterrupted to the present time.

4. That they have been always printed for the use of The House, and expressly for publication and sale.

5. That the Reports and Parliamentary Papers have likewise been printed for the use of The House, and expressly for publication; and from a very early period were authorised to be sold.

25 February 1837. *James & Luke G. Hansard & Sons.*

II.—SUMMARY STATEMENT.

Publication and Circulation of Parliamentary Papers, 1731 to 1836.

Publication and Circulation, 1731—1836.

The particulars relating to this subject before the Union with Ireland, are obscure and difficult to collect.

The earliest date of any Paper in our stores is 1731. From that year to 1796, the number of copies remaining on hand in 1807, varies from 6 to 50, and of some Reports 200 or 300. From these instances it may be concluded that the same power was then, as now, exercised, of apportioning the number of copies printed, not only to the supply of Members for their use only, but for distribution to the public.

From 1797, the means of information are more certain; and the particulars about to be stated, are furnished by documents in our possession.

At this period, the general or minimum number of copies printed was 500, the number of Members being 558.

The circulation and publication to a certain extent may be inferred from the number of copies printed exceeding the number of Members, and a similar inference may be made of an extra circulation from the extra number of copies printed of particular Papers.

Thus in 1797-8, the number of articles ordered by The House to be printed was 104; of 91 of which 500 copies were printed, and of 13, from 600 to 1,200 copies. See Paper (1 A.)

In 1798-9, the number of articles ordered by The House was 90: of 76 of which 500 copies were printed, and of 14, from 600 to 1,000 copies. See Paper (1 B.)

In 1799-1800, the number of articles ordered by The House was 121: of 104 of which 500 copies were printed, and of 17, from 600 to 1,500 copies. See Paper (1 C.)

In 1801, the first year of the Union, the number of Members being 658, an increase was made in the general number of copies printed, the minimum number being 650. The number of articles ordered by The House was 145: of 134 of which 650 copies were printed, and of 11, from 850 to 1,000. See Paper (1 D.)

In 1802, the number of articles ordered by The House was 132: of 121 of which 650 copies were printed and of 11, from 800 to 1,500 copies. See Paper (1 E.)

In 1805, the number of articles ordered by The House was 231: of 182 of which 650 copies were printed, and of 53, from 800 to 1,550. See Paper (1 F.)

In 1809, the general number of copies was increased to 750. The number of articles ordered by The House was 282: of 171 of which 750 copies were printed, and of 111, from 1,000 to 1,750. See Paper (1 G.)

In 1814-15, the general number of copies was increased to 850.

In 1816, the general number was increased to 900.

In 1819-20, the general number was increased to 1,000, at which it remains.

In 1824, the number of articles ordered by The House was 479: of 391 of which 1,000 copies were printed; of 69, from 1,250 to 1,750; and of 19, from 2,000 to 5,000. See Paper (1 H.)

In 1825, the number of articles ordered by The House was 523: of 419 of which 1,000 copies were printed; of 155, from 1,250 to 1,750; and of 25, from 2,000 to 8,000. See Paper (1 I.)

Appendix, No. 9.

See Paper 4, p. 84 post.

Extensive circulation has been frequently given to Reports and Papers investigating important subjects, to Accounts of statistical facts, and to Bills affecting the laws on great commercial or constitutional questions, the authority for such circulation being invariably given by The Speaker; and the mode of transmission has been by the General Post, free as Parliamentary proceedings, except when the packages have been of considerable bulk, in which case the expense of carriage has been paid by the Government. In some cases the circulation has been effected by individuals, either Members of Parliament who have been Chairmen of the Committees which have investigated the subject of the Reports or Papers, or other Members, officers in public departments, or individuals who have interested themselves in the subjects of the inquiries carried on, or in the operation of the laws proposed to be altered. But in every case the authority of The Speaker has been required to sanction the circulation.

Besides this description of circulation for direct public purposes, very numerous instances have occurred in the last 10 years of applications to The Speaker, in some cases for numbers of copies of particular Papers, and in very many instances for selections of Papers on given subjects. These have been supplied at the cost of the public, as well of the Papers, as of the expense of selecting them from the stores, and arranging them in subjects.

The following Account will show the extent of these applications for four years.

In 1833, the number of copies delivered out of store on these Orders was	8,000
In 1834-35 - - - - - - - - - - -	14,000
In 1835 - - - - - - - - - - - -	44,107
In 1836 { By Speaker's Order, 18,454 / By Sale - - 29,716 } - - - - - - -	48,1[illegible]

FACILITIES afforded to getting Information of the PARLIAMENTARY PAPERS, and which may have contributed to their Increased Circulation since 1801.

1. By the arranging the Papers in volumes, with contents (which was first done in 1803); and placing them in several public libraries.
2. By the Annual Indexes, which were first introduced in 1814.
3. By the General Index, from 1801 to 1826, which was compiled in 1829, and enlarged in 1832.
4. By the Annual List of Papers, numerically arranged, which commenced in 1833.
5. By the Catalogues, from 1696 to 1834, compiled in 1834.
6. By the Notices of Sessional Papers and Sale Lists issued in 1836.

PUBLICATION and CIRCULATION of PARLIAMENTARY PAPERS, after and in furtherance of the Resolution for the Sale.

The Resolution of the House was made in August 1835, and came into operation at the commencement of the ensuing Session in February 1836. The necessary arrangements and the rate of prices were made and adjusted by the Committee for assisting The Speaker in directing the printing, in March.

Three Offices for Sale were opened:

1. Adjoining the Waiting Room in the House of Commons, for the accommodation of Members only.
2. In Abingdon-street, for the use of persons attending on Parliament.
3. In Great Turnstile, adjoining the Printing-office, for general use; but chiefly for members of the legal profession, and persons resorting to the Inns of Court, and for the town and country trade.
4. Agencies were appointed in Edinburgh and Dublin.

Every suitable information was given to the public of the accommodation afforded for procuring the Parliamentary Papers;

1. By Advertisements in the principal Newspapers.
2. By Notifications hung up in the Lobbies of the House.
3. By Special Notifications of Reports on such subjects as have, from time to time, come under the discussion of Committees.
4. By Lists of the Titles of the Papers, with the prices affixed.

The progress of the Sale is exhibited in the subjoined Account, by which it appears that, in the first year of its operation, upwards of 29,700 copies of Bills, Reports and Accounts have been, by that means, issued to the public.

27 February 1837.

James & Luke G. Hansard & Sons.

PAPERS REFERRED TO.

— 1. —

STATEMENT of the NUMBER of COPIES printed for the use of The House and for Circulation. — Number of Copies Printed.

(A.)

1797–8.

Number of Articles ordered by The House	104
General number of Copies printed of each	600

(Members 558.)

Extra Copies printed of the following Articles:—

Report, Committee of Secrecy	1,000	Report on Supply	800
Bill, Assessed Taxes	1,900	Report, Scotch Distilleries	800
Bill, Defence of the Royal Person	1,000	Report, Fisheries	800
Bill, Land Tax	2,000		

(B.)

1798–9.

Number of Articles ordered by The House	90
General number of Copies printed of each	600

Extra Copies printed of the following Articles:—

Bill, Duties	1,500	Report, Wet Docks	800
Bill, Fisheries	800	Report, Copper Trade	800
Account, East India Company	800	Bill, Wet Docks	800
Propositions, Union	1,000	Report, London Port	800
Report, Committee of Secrecy	1,800	Bengal Papers	800
Report, Fisheries	800	Imports and Exports	800
Report, Port of London	800	Report, Distilleries	800

(C.)

1799–1800.

Number of Articles ordered by The House	111
General number of Copies printed of each	650

Extra Copies printed of the following Articles:—

Bill, Volunteers	1,100	Bill, Provisions	1,000
Paper, East India	800	Bill, Income Duties	600
Ditto	600	Report, Bills of Inclosure	800
Account, East India	800	Report, Wool	800
Report, High Price of Provisions	1,000	Bill, Income	700
Second Report, ditto	1,000	Report, Trade	800
Resolutions, Union	1,200	Revenue Accounts	800
Bill, Mills Regulation	1,000	Report, Public Revenue	1,600

(D.)

1801.

Number of Articles ordered by The House	146
General number of Copies printed of each	650

(Members 658.)

Extra Copies printed of the following Articles:—

Report, Provisions	1,000	Report, Port of London	1,000
Ditto - ditto	1,000	Accounts, East India Company	850
Report, Committee of Secrecy	850	Papers - ditto	850
No. 64.—Accounts, East India Company	850	Report, Provisions	1,000
Report, Committee of Secrecy	1,000	Report, Salt Duties	1,000
Report, Provisions	1,000		

(E.)

1802.

Number of Articles ordered by The House - - - - - - - - 152
General number of Copies printed of each - - - - - - - 650

Extra Copies printed of the following Articles :—

Population - - - - - -	1,000	Bill, Apprentices - - - - -	1,000
Report, Civil List - - - -	800	Bill, Militia - - - - - -	750
Report, Corn Trade - - - -	1,000	Bill, Fisheries - - - - -	600
Bill, Export of Grain - - - -	700	Accounts, East India Company - -	800
Bill, Clergy Residence - - - -	1,500	Paper - ditto - - - - -	800
Bill, Militia - - - - - -	1,500		

(F.)

1804.

Number of Articles ordered by The House - - - - - - - - 191
General number of Copies printed of each - - - - - - - 650

Extra Copies printed of the following Articles :—

Report, Naval Inquiry - - - -	1,400	Bill, Small Debts - - - - -	800
Ditto - ditto - - - -	1,400	Bill, Seamen - - - - - -	684
Account, British Museum - - -	800	Report, Duke of Athol - - - -	1,000
Finance Accounts - - - -	1,000	Report, Highland Roads - - - -	1,400
Report, Chalmers and Cowie's Claim -	700	Report, Duke of Athol - - - -	1,000
Bill, Smuggling - - - - -	800	Report, Naval Inquiry - - - -	1,500
Papers, Isle of Man - - - -	1,000	Report, Lord Melville - - - -	1,100
Bill, Property Tax - - - -	1,000	Report, Caledonian Canal - - -	1,400
Report, Naval Inquiry - - - -	1,400	Accounts, Ships of War - - -	1,000
Finance Accounts - - - -	1,000	Corn Trade - - - - - -	1,000
Report, Naval Inquiry - - - -	1,650	Report, Ship Romney - - - -	1,000
Bill, Estimates, Seamen - - -	800	Report, Romney - - - - -	1,000
Papers, Romney - - - - -	800	Accounts, Dock Yards - - - -	1,000
Naval Inquiry - - - - -	1,400	Two Papers, ditto - - - -	1,000
Comptroller of the Navy - - -	1,400	Report, East India Company - -	850
Naval Inquiry - - - - -	1,400	Report, Naval Inquiry - - - -	1,000
Romney Papers - - - - -	800	Papers, Navy Board - - - -	1,000
Ditto - - - - - - -	800	Bill, Pilots - - - - - -	1,000

(G.)

1809.

Number of Articles ordered by The House - - - - - - - - [illegible]
General number of Copies printed of each - - - - - - - 750

Extra Copies printed of the following Articles :—

Military Inquiry - - - - -	1,500	Report, Turnpike Roads - - -	1,000
Ditto - - - - - - -	1,500	Report, Public Expenditure - -	1,750
Bill, Militia - - - - - -	1,000	Three Papers, Portugal - - -	1,000
Three Accounts, ditto - - - -	1,000	Bill, Revenue, Scotland - - -	1,000
Barracks, Return - - - - -	1,000	Accounts, Admiralty - - - -	1,000
Regular Army, ditto - - - -	1,000	Report, Cotton Weavers - - -	1,000
Two Accounts, Militia - - - -	1,000	Sir J. Moore - - - - -	1,000
Report, Foss - - - - - -	1,500	Report, Ardglass Harbour - - -	800
Papers, Portugal - - - - -	1,000	Papers, Isle of Capri - - -	800
Orders in Council - - - - -	1,000	Two Papers, Portugal - - - -	1,000
Duke of York - - - - - -	1,000	Nine Reports, Naval Affairs - -	1,500
Account, Spirits - - - - -	1,000	Papers, Portugal - - - - -	1,000
Carnatic Debts - - - - -	1,000	Papers, Spain - - - - -	1,000
Four Army Returns - - - -	1,000	Two Reports, Windsor Forest - -	800
Finance Accounts - - - - -	1,000	Report, Military Inquiry - - -	1,000
Commissariat - - - - - -	1,000	Report, Education, Ireland - -	750
Two Returns, Army Correspondence -	1,000	Two Papers, Portugal - - - -	1,000
America, Diplomatic Paper - - -	1,000	Report, Highland Roads - - -	1,400
Paper, Chesapeake - - - - -	1,000	Report, Land Revenue - - - -	1,000
Report, Ordnance - - - - -	1,500	Bill, Sees, Ireland - - - -	800
Papers, America - - - - -	1,000	Papers, Spain - - - - -	1,000
Two Papers, Spain - - - -	1,000	Five Papers, Army - - - -	1,000
Public Records - - - - -	1,250	Report, Imports and Exports - -	1,000
Bill, Militia - - - - - -	850	Report, Public Expenditure - -	1,750
Three Papers, Spain - - - -	1,000	Bill, Purity of Parliament - - -	800
Finance Accounts - - - - -	1,000	Papers, East India Company - -	850
Army Correspondence - - - -	1,000	Accounts, Clergy Residence - -	1,000
Report, East India Company - -	1,000	Ditto, Queen Anne's Bounty - -	1,000
Five Papers, Spain and Portugal - -	1,000	Report, Broad Wheels - - - -	1,000

Accounts, Clergy	1,000	Report, Telford's Survey	1,000
Report, Caledonian Canal	1,400	Report, Broad Wheels	1,000
Two Accounts, Army	1,000	Accounts, East India Affairs	850
Papers, East India Affairs	850	Bill, Stage Coaches	1,000
Report, Prisons	1,000	Bill, Turnpike Trusts	1,000
Papers, East India Affairs	850		

(H.)

1834.

Number of Articles ordered by The House - - - - - - - 470

General number of Copies printed of each - - - - - - - 1,000

Extra Copies printed:

Above 1,000 and not exceeding 1,250 of - - - - - - 40 Articles.

From 1,500 to 1,750 of - - - - - - - - - - 29 —

From 2,000 to 5,000 of - - - - - - - - - - 19 Articles, viz.:

Treadwheels, Correspondence	2,500	Education, Ireland	2,000
Artizans and Machinery	2,000	Slave Insurrections	2,250
Bank, Papers	4,000	Ditto	2,250
Ditto, Four per cents	5,000	Education, Ireland	2,000
Charity Report	2,500	Ditto	2,000
Education, Ireland	2,000	Poor Rates, Report	2,500
Vaccine Report	11,000	Salmon, Report	2,000
Scotch Appeals, Report	2,250	Foreign Trade, Report	2,500
Treadwheels	2,500	Charities, Report	2,500
Constabulary Paper	2,000		

(I.)

1835.

Number of Articles ordered by The House - - - - - - - 633

General number of Copies printed of each - - - - - - - 1,000

Extra Copies printed:

1,250 to 1,750 of - - - - - - - - - - - 153 Articles.

2,000 to 3,000 of - - - - - - - - - - - 35 —

Private Bill List	1,500	Corporations, England	1,500
Small Debts Bill	1,600	Statute Law, Report	2,500
Education, Abstracts	2,500	Turnpike Roads, Bill	2,500
Highland Roads and Bridges	1,750	Prisons, Four Reports	2,500
Marriages Bill	1,500	Poor Rate Account	2,500
Church Temporalities Report	2,000	Education, England, Report	1,500
Corporation Reform, England	2,500	Colonial Expenditure, Report	1,500
Ditto	2,500	British Museum, Report	2,000
Slavery Papers	1,500	Handloom Weavers, Report	2,500
Imprisonment for Debt Bill	1,500	Canada, Report	1,500
County Rates Report	2,000	Poor Laws, Report	3,000
Charities Report	2,500	Sinecures, Report	2,000
Criminal Offenders Accounts	3,000	Timber Trade, Report	2,500
Highland Churches Report	2,000	Bribery, Report	2,500
Corporations, Bill	2,750	Holyhead, Report	1,750
Court of Session, Bill	1,500	Public Works, Report	1,500
Poor Rates, Abstract	2,500	General Darling, Report	2,000
Public Works, Ireland	1,500	Slave Papers	1,500
Handloom Weavers, Report	2,500	Arts and Manufactures, Report	2,000
Connaught Lakes, Report	1,500	Accidents in Mines, Report	1,500
Ecclesiastical Revenues, Bill	1,500	Orange Institutions, Report	2,000
Poor, Ireland, Report	3,000	New Churches, Report	1,750
Gurney's Steam Carriages	1,500	Woods and Forests, Report	1,750
Three Reports, Orange Lodges	2,000		

— 2. —

INSTANCES OF EXTENSIVE CIRCULATION.

1800. The Report of the Committee on Records was circulated to the public libraries and to many individuals interested in the subject.

The Population Abstracts were circulated to the public libraries, clerks of the peace, and other public officers throughout the kingdom, in 1801, 1811, 1821 and 1831.

1816. The Charitable Donations Returns were extensively circulated.

1822. 1,750 Copies of the Supplement to the Poor Rate Returns were circulated to individuals as Parliamentary proceedings.

1824. A complete set of Parliamentary Papers, from 1818 to 1821, making 64 volumes, to the Faculty of Advocates, Edinburgh.

One hundred and forty-six Copies of Jurors' Qualification Bill, to clerks of the peace, &c.

Three hundred and twenty-four Copies of Report on Scotch Appeals, to law officers, &c. in Scotland.

Ninety-six Copies of Scotch Judicature Bill, to law officers in Scotland, as Parliamentary proceedings.

Reports on Courts of Justice, Scotland; Scotch Judicature Bill, and Scotch Small Debts Bill, to county clerks of Scotland, as Parliamentary proceedings.

Three hundred Copies of Scotch Appeals, to J. Hope, Edinburgh, for circulation.

The National Vaccine Report, generally circulated throughout the United Kingdom, to the clergy, magistrates, clerks of the peace, and official persons.

Twenty-six Copies of Reports and Papers respecting the Courts of Justice, Ireland, to C. W. Wynn, Esq., for circulation.

1825. Fifty Copies of Accounts relating to Iron and Tin, to Mr. Littleton.

Fifty Copies of Wrongous Imprisonment Bill, to Mr. Grant, for circulation.

Four hundred Copies of Report, Education in Ireland, to Mr. Pennefather, for circulation in Ireland.

Thirty Copies Reports on Friendly Societies.

Thirty Copies Poor Rate Returns.

Thirty Copies ditto Supplement, to Mr. Courtenay, for distribution.

Four hundred Copies of Appendix to First Report on Education, Ireland, to Mr. Pennefather, for distribution in Ireland.

1831. 1,650 Copies of Accounts of Local Taxation, circulated as Parliamentary proceedings.

1835. Report on Poor Laws, 1,348 Copies, circulated by post.

One hundred Copies of Imprisonment for Debt Bill, as Parliamentary proceedings.

27 February 1837.

Jas. & Luke G. Hansard & Sons.

Appendix, No. 4.

Extracts from Reports.

Appendix, No. 4.

EXTRACTS from REPORTS of COMMITTEES of the HOUSE of COMMONS, of OPINIONS, RECOMMENDATIONS, EVIDENCE and STATEMENTS, respecting the Ordering of the PRINTING, DISTRIBUTION, and SALE of REPORTS and PARLIAMENTARY PAPERS.

— 1. —

Ninth Report on Public Expenditure; 20 June 1810. (373.)

The Votes of the House of Commons are printed by Mr. Nichols, who has executed this work for many years. Rep. 1810 (373.) p. 179.

The number of copies printed in 1808 was 936, the excess above 750 being sold and credit given for them in account. Since the year 1803 various alterations have been introduced from time to time, consisting chiefly in the compression of some entries, and in the increase of the quantity of the letter-press contained in each page. These improvements were introduced through the very careful and accurate attention of Mr. Speaker.

The Journals and the miscellaneous Papers of the House of Commons, including Bills and Reports, are printed by Mr. Hansard. A similar economy has been extended to them, they having also been subjected to Mr. Speaker's general superintendence.

The number of copies of miscellaneous Papers printed is in each instance directed by Mr. Speaker, and has, since the Union with Ireland, been generally from 750 to 1,200 or 1,500, and in some few instances, much larger. p. 180.

Evidence.

Geo. Whittam, Esq. Clerk of the Journals & Papers. p. 194.

Please to state what course you take in respect to the Votes?—The Votes are ordered to be printed at the commencement of every Session, being first perused by The Speaker, who is to appoint the printing thereof; and the printing has been conducted by the same printing office for a great length of time, the elder Mr. Nichols (who is now one of the printers) having been employed on them in the year 1787.

What number of these are printed?—In 1808, 936 copies were printed, 750 of which were delivered to the Vote Office on the public account; and the rest were sold by Messrs. Nichols for 86 *l.* 4 *s.* 6 *d.* (as they state), for which sum credit is given by them in their account of printing for that Session.

What is the course that you take in respect to the miscellaneous Papers ordered to be printed by The House, and what are the number of them?—When The House order Papers to be printed, I send them to press with the greatest possible expedition, and generally take The Speaker's directions as to the number of copies to be printed, either verbally or in writing; 600 copies was the number generally printed before the Union with Ireland took place; the number was then increased to 650, and if no particular order was given for an extra number, that was the quantity of all Papers printed; but in some cases the numbers were increased to 800, 1,000, 1,200, or 1,500, and in some few instances to a larger number, according to the order of The Speaker. p. 195.

With respect to the distribution, I have in my hand a paper signed by The Speaker, and dated the 1st of April 1802, directing Mr. Hansard to send such a number of copies to the Vote Office, for the use of the Members, &c. as are here specified.

Out of			
650	to	send	600
800	-	-	700
1,000	-	-	800
1,200 or 1,500	-	-	1,000

or a larger number upon receiving a further order; and these directions have been followed from that period till the beginning of the present Session.

A representation having been made to The Speaker, from the Vote office, in the course of the last Session, that there were not a sufficient number of copies printed of the miscellaneous Papers to supply the Members and other persons entitled thereto, The Speaker, in October last, gave directions through me to the Vote office to make out a fair list of the distribution of such portion of copies as were delivered to them, viz. for The Speaker, Officers

Appendix, No. 4.

Evidence.

Geo. Whittam, Esq. Clerk of the Journals & Papers.

Rep. 1810 (373.)

p. 194.

Officers of the House, Members and Public Offices, &c. in England, Scotland and Ireland; and the Vote office thereupon delivered such list to The Speaker, and a copy thereof to me, which I now produce, dated 14th November 1808; [*delivered in*]; and in consequence of The Speaker's considering that the number of 650 did not appear by such list sufficient to answer the demand at the Vote office, and to make a reserve of some copies for the use of The House, directions were given by him to print 750 copies of Papers in general, and to send to the Vote office, out of 750 or 800 copies, 658; and of 1,000 or upwards, 900; or a larger number upon receiving a further order.

The Speaker occasionally directs a larger number to be printed (as I have already mentioned), according to the degree of publicity which it appears to him was intended by The House to be given to such Papers, and the nature of their contents.

On giving directions for printing an extra number of Reports and other Papers, The Speaker has often stated to me, that regard should be had to the probability of such Papers being required at some future time for the use of The House, or any Committee thereof, in which case it would be more economical to print at first an extra number of copies for such purpose, incurring thereby only the additional cost of paper for the additional copies; and preventing the further expense as well as the delay of re-printing them when called for.

Messrs. Hansard, p. 203.

I wish to say, in addition to my former evidence, that I never altered the mode of printing without authority, nor increased the usual numbers without the authority of The Speaker.

— 2. —

Report on Printing and Stationery, 30 *July* 1822. (607.)

Evidence.

Messrs. Hansard. p. 198.

WILL you explain to the Committee the reason of the apparently very large disproportion between the reams of paper that were printed in 1818 and 1819?—In 1818, the number of copies of the majority of the papers printed was only 750, varying in some cases to 1,000, and in some few cases to a greater number; in 1819, the number of copies was generally 1,000, and in many cases they were much more, and in some instances very large numbers were printed, 1,500, 1,750, 2,000, and even 3,500; of course a greater quantity of paper was used.

By whose order was that disproportionate number ordered?—By The Speaker's order. I always apply to The Speaker for directions for the number of copies to be printed.

Does The Speaker make the order in writing to you, when he varies the number that are to be printed of any particular paper?—I write upon the proof, "how many copies to be printed," and The Speaker puts the number, with his initials underneath it, where it exceeds 1,000.

In what way is the general order issued to you as to the general number, where not varied; in writing, or how?—By the clerk of the Journals.

Verbally?—Yes; he receives The Speaker's direction, and he communicates it to me.

p. 200.

What receipts do you obtain for papers delivered to any individual; do you take any receipts?—No; I deliver none without The Speaker's order. When I say to no individual, I should explain, that if an honourable Member were to call on me and say he wanted a bill or paper pending in Parliament, I should be thought particularly if I were to refuse to deliver it; but no important paper or volume of Journals is delivered without an order.

Mr. J. B. Nichols.

p. 206.

Your Father and yourself print the Votes of the House of Commons?—Yes.

Are there any observations which you wish to make to the Committee with regard to printing the Votes?—In expectation that I should be called upon, I have taken the liberty of putting down two or three observations upon that subject. The printers of the Votes beg leave most respectfully to state, that Mr. Nichols, the elder, has had the satisfaction to be employed, as printer of the Votes, for above sixty years, and his son above twenty-five years; that from the year 1769 to 1777, the Votes were printed by J. Nichols, senior, and his predecessor, Mr. Bowyer; and that they, after deducting the expenses, accounted to The Speaker for the profit, which from 1755 to 1772, amounted on an average to about 240*l.* a year.

Are the Committee to understand, that from the year 1755 to the year 1772, the Members were supplied with copies of the Votes, and that the public were put to no expense for the same?—Yes; 600 copies were delivered gratis to the House of Commons.

Were the Votes sold to the public at that time?—Yes; it was from the extra sale that all the expenses were paid for printing the 600 delivered to The House, and the printing those that were sold; there was still a profit after paying the expenses. From 1772, the sale gradually diminished (occasioned by the proceedings of The House being regularly detailed in the newspapers), till in 1777 there was an actual loss, when the then Speaker, Sir Fletcher Norton, transferred the account to the Treasury. Since that period, the printer's bill has been regularly certified by The Speaker at the end of each Session, and the balance has been received from the Treasury.

p. 207.

What number of the Votes is usually sold?—About 200 copies each day.

How is that brought to the account?—That is deducted from my account.

How

Appendix, No. 4.

Evidence.

Mr. J. B. Nichols, p. 907. Rep. 1826 (607.)

How many of the Appendixes are sold?—I do not think any are sold, at least not latterly.

How many copies of the Votes and Appendix do you print in all?—1,175 of the Votes, and 1,000 of the Appendix.

Are those sold at the Vote office included in that number?—Yes, they are; I have here a statement of the delivery of Votes.

[*The witness delivered in the same, which was read, as follows*:]

" Delivery of the Votes:

" On the morning of publication, there are delivered to Mr. Mitchell, of the Vote-office, on the public account, for the use of the Members and public offices, &c. - 900
Also, for sale by Mr. Mitchell, who supplies the public demand for the Votes - 200
Afterwards delivered to Mr. Mitchell, to be kept in store - - - - - 75

Total printed - - - 1,175 "

— 3. —

Report on the State of Printed Reports and Papers; 1 *July* 1825. (516.)

Your Committee recommend, that at the close of every Session complete sets of the printed Papers should be deposited in the Library of the *British Museum*, the *Bodleian* and *Cambridge* University Library, the Library of *Trinity College*, *Dublin*, and the Advocates' Library at *Edinburgh*. Report, p. 4.

— 4. —

Report on the King's Printers' Patents; 8 *August* 1832. (713.)

Appendix (C.) to 1, p. 318.

LIST of SETS of SESSIONAL PAPERS, done up in Volumes, and delivered at the end of each Session.

The Right Hon. The Speaker - - - - - - - - - - 1 set.
The Right Hon. The First Lord of the Treasury - - - - - - - 1 set.
The Three Lords of the Treasury - - - - - - - - - 3 sets.
The Right Hon. The Chancellor of the Exchequer - - - - - - 2 sets.
Ditto - - - - - Ditto - - - - - for Ireland - - - - - - 1 set.
The Two Secretaries of the Treasury - - - - - - - - 2 sets.
The Assistant Secretary of the Treasury - - - - - - - - 1 set.
The Speaker's Gallery - - - - - - - - - - - - 1 set.
The Speaker's Secretary - - - - - - - - - - - 1 set.
The Clerk of the Journals and Papers - - - - - - - - 1 set.
Ditto - - Ditto - - for the Office - - - - - - - - 1 set.
The Committee Rooms - - - - - - - - - - - - 2 sets.
The House of Commons Library - - - - - - - - - - 1 set.
The Lords' Library - - - - - - - - - - - - - 1 set.
The Clerk of the Parliamentary Accounts, Treasury - - - - - - 1 set.
The Solicitors to the Treasury - - - - - - - - - - 1 set.
The Secretary of State, Home Department - - - - - - - - 1 set.
Ditto - - - Foreign - Ditto - - - - - - - - - 1 set.
Ditto - - - Colonial - Ditto - - - - - - - - - 1 set.
The Office of Privy Council - - - - - - - - - - - 1 set.
The Office of Woods and Forests - - - - - - - - - - 1 set.
The Army Pay Office - - - - - - - - - - - - 1 set.
The Revenue Board - - - - - - - - - - - - - 1 set.
The British Museum - - - - - - - - - - - - 1 set.
The Bodleian Library - - - - - - - - - - - - 1 set.
The University, Cambridge - - - - - - - - - - - 1 set.
The Library at Trinity College, Dublin - - - - - - - - 1 set.
The Advocates' Library, Edinburgh - - - - - - - - - 1 set.
The Vote Office, House of Commons - - - - - - - - - 1 set.
The Chamber of Deputies (France) - - - - - - - - - 1 set.
Belgian Chamber of Deputies - - - - - - - - - - 1 set.
Bavarian Library at Munich - - - - - - - - - - - 1 set.

Printing Office, 23 Nov. 1831.

James & Luke G. Hansard & Sons.

Evidence.

— 5. —

Report on Printing done for The House; 10 July 1828. (510.)

J. H. Ley, Esq. Clerk of the House. p. 12. Rep. 1828 (510)

HAVE you observed of late any difference in the manner in which Petitions are drawn up and presented to the House, beyond the common mode of praying for some relief?—There are many cases of Petitions which are more like pamphlets than Petitions; where persons wish to give their sentiments to the public through the medium of Petitions to the House of Commons, instead of printing what they have to say in pamphlets. I yesterday saw a Petition which is to be presented to the House of Commons, respecting the office of a justice of the peace, which is precisely of this description.

In printing these Petitions how does it give a circulation to them beyond the Members? — Many people buy the Votes.

Who orders the quantity of the copies to be printed of the Votes and the Appendix?—There are enough printed for the Members, and a certain number of extra copies, according to what the sale is.

Is it regulated by what is supposed to be the demand for them by the Public, or simply for the use of the Members?—There are a certain number for the use of the Members, and to be kept in store; and I believe the Printer prints as many as he can get sale for; but the farther details upon that subject may be obtained from Mr. Mitchell.

p. 13. Is not the number of Papers printed for the use of the House of Commons under the direction of The Speaker?—I think 1,000 copies is the number, if there is no other direction given; if it is a Paper of any consequence, The Speaker gives directions according to what he considers necessary; sometimes 1,500 to 2,000, or 2,500.

Do you know whether the expense of printing these Papers is charged to the Public, or any individual?—It is all charged to the Public; there are no Papers sold except the Votes.

John Bull, Esq. Clerk of the Journals & Papers. p. 17.

Is there any regulated number of each Paper that is ordered to be printed?—No; not exactly so; the number generally printed is 1,000; but if more are required, it is always done by an order from The Speaker to me, giving directions for an additional number; and that must depend upon the supposed utility of the Paper for general information.

p. 19. Are not the Papers of the House sold by the *Printer* to the Public in considerable numbers, independent of those furnished for the accommodation of Members of the House?—Certainly not a single copy, to my knowledge; but there is the proper person to answer to that.

All the clubs are supplied with them?—I am not aware of that fact; but if they are, it is not through the Printer; they may be supplied in a variety of ways.

Explain how.—There are eight or ten or a dozen copies that belong to messengers and others about the House, but whom I do not know, who sell their copies; I believe many copies Members take away themselves. The great quantity of Papers that get into other people's hands are the gifts of Members, as I believe. My answer referred to Papers presented to the House of Commons, Accounts and Miscellaneous Papers; but the Appendix to the Votes, and the Votes themselves, are sold by authority; and part of the money is brought to account.

Does that money brought to account pay the additional expense that is incurred in providing this additional number of Votes or Petitions?—I should say certainly not; but the Printer of the Votes, and the person who is employed to deliver them, and who is also the person authorized to sell them, are the proper persons to give that information to the Committee.

Messrs. *Hansard*. p. 28.

Do you generally reprint the same number of copies printed originally?—The usual number is 1,000, and generally when a reprint takes place the same number is printed; 1,000 is the general number, but there are frequently larger impressions.

One thousand is the general order under which you generally act?—Yes, certainly, that is the general number.

Of all Papers?—Yes.

That being a larger number than is distributed among the Members of the House of Commons, what becomes of the surplus?—We deliver to the Vote Office for distribution to the Members, 913; 33 are delivered to the chief Officers of the House and the Treasury, and 57 remain to be put up into consecutive sets; at the end of the Session they are delivered to the Library of the House of Commons, to the Treasury, and certain public Offices, and 17 copies remain in our store; subject to orders from The Speaker to deliver to Members as they apply for them; they, by the accumulation of many years, form a great collection, and a considerable increase of our cares and responsibility. In larger numbers, a similar distribution takes place, greater in proportion to the Vote Office, leaving in our store in some cases 167 copies, and in larger impressions, sometimes 400 copies, and generally the largest number that remains in our store of any particular Paper is from 400 to 500.

Mr. *James Mitchell*. p. 31.

WHAT situation do you hold in the House of Commons?—Deliverer of Votes and Printed Papers.

Will you state to the Committee the business that appertains to your office, as to the receiving and delivering of the Votes?—I receive them every day as they are printed, from the Printer, and send them out every morning to the Members.

What

Appendix, No. 4.

Evidence.

Mr. James Mitchell.

p. 31.

Rep. 1828 (520.)

What are you paid by each Member?—My charge is two guineas and a half per session.

That is the charge for the delivery of the Papers?—The Votes and Papers.

What number of the Votes do you generally receive?—Nine hundred.

Is that a regulated number?—It is.

Is there any regulated number of Papers printed which you receive, or is that number accidental?—The regular number received by me of each Paper is 900, but of some particular Papers that number is increased.

Receiving so many more numbers of copies than can be wanted for the use of the Members, what becomes of the surplus number of copies?—The surplus copies are kept in store; but although it might appear that a very large surplus must remain from the number received by me, yet when the Committee are informed that, in addition to 658 Members, there are the Public Offices, Officers and Libraries in England, Ireland and Scotland, Clerks, Door-keepers and Messengers of The House who are entitled to them, that apparent surplus will be much decreased. Many Members likewise require copies for their use in The House, and also send two, three or more copies of particular Papers to their constituents. The Speaker also gives orders.

How many copies does that take?—I think nearly forty Officers and Clerks of The House, and the others amount to above a hundred.

When you say they are entitled to them, you mean that they get them for nothing?—Yes, they are entitled to them by long-established usage; I do not know how it arose.

Are the remaining copies that are left in your office, after the Members and Clerks of The House are supplied, sold or disposed of, or what becomes of them?—They are kept in store; there are only a certain number of copies sold, which I sell.

How many are sold?—Upwards of seventy copies.

At what rate are they sold?—Eight guineas and a half, including the delivery.

Do you account for any part of that which is received for the Papers?—No, only to the individuals of whom I buy them.

Of whom do you buy them?—The Clerks and Officers of The House.

You buy of the Messengers and Officers of The House those Papers which are delivered to them from established usage?—Yes, just so.

Are there any Papers or Votes sold by you in your office for which you account to the Public?—Yes, Votes a certain number; but not of Papers.

Describe what you mean by Papers?—Reports, Returns and Accounts, and all Papers laid on the table of The House which are printed.

What is the amount of money which you receive for the Votes for which you account to the Public?—I think my bill to the Printer for Votes last year was about 500*l.*; I receive 900 copies of Votes; beyond that number, any I may want, I pay for to the Printer, and he accounts to The House for them.

At what rate do you pay for them?—Three-pence per sheet; the public pay me three guineas a set for the Votes and Proceedings as delivered every morning. I pay the Printer whatever they may come to at three-pence per sheet.

The Votes you speak of, are those printed by Mr. Nichols?—Yes.

Do you pay the same for the Papers printed by Mr. Hansard?—No; I purchase nothing of Mr. Hansard.

From whom do you purchase the different Papers printed by Mr. Hansard?—Of the Door-keepers and Messengers, and other persons entitled to receive them.

If there were a greater demand for Papers of that kind than you could get from the supply to which you are accustomed to apply, could you get them from the printing-office?—No, not a sheet of any sort or kind; of the number supplied to the Public, some are those which Members give me; other Members take their Votes, and instead of paying the usual demand for sending them, give me their Papers.

How many persons are employed in delivering them?—There are ten, besides my deputy, and three clerks. By so many being employed, the Members get their Votes and Papers delivered early in the morning to all parts of London.

Is the sale of the Papers to those persons considered a part of the emoluments of your office?—Yes, towards the expenses of the office.

Is there any allowance made to you from any other source for the keeping of that office?—None, but a salary which I receive of 14*l.* 11*s.* 6*d.* to pay myself, deputy and thirteen persons.

You say you receive 900 copies of all Papers and Votes; how many do you deliver on an average regularly daily to the different Members?—I should think about 630 at this time in town and country; there are some Members who have them sent regularly into the country.

The whole of the Members are in the habit of receiving those Papers?—Not all of them, as I have before stated.

On an average throughout the Session, do you imagine you issue 500 complete copies of Papers and Votes daily?—Yes, certainly, more.

You have stated that on an average you deliver about 630 copies of Papers and Votes to the Members of The House?—Yes.

That forty copies are the perquisites of the Officers of The House; that there are then upwards of 250 copies a surplus in your office; do the whole of those remain in store?—The number in store is always uncertain, as it depends on the application of Members for extra copies, and The Speaker's orders.

How many are delivered to the Public Offices?—I think between fifty and sixty.

Appendix, No. 4.

Evidence:

Mr. James Mitchell, p. 31. Rep. 1828 (520.)

That would still leave about 250?—Yes, of some things; but, as I have before stated, the number is always uncertain.

Any Member requiring any particular Paper for transmission into the country, are you in the habit of giving it to him?—Certainly.

A Member occasionally asking for a second copy of any Report, you are in the habit of giving it?—Yes.

Do you conceive you could sell an additional number of the Papers and Votes at the same price as you make your sales, provided they were sent you?—The sale of the Votes being unlimited, whatever number might be required would be supplied; the Papers, although limited, I should think at present sufficient.

Have you any further information to give to the Committee upon the subject of delivering the Votes, which might tend in any manner to lessen the expense attendant upon it? —I am not aware of any.

Have you any store where the surplus Papers are lodged?—Yes.

Is there a great quantity of them?—Yes, of some things; of others but few, and of some none.

Do you consider yourself authorized to deliver out of your store, without the authority of The Speaker, after the end of the year?—Yes, to Members, one or two copies; but if a larger number be required, The Speaker's order must be obtained; and if my store will not allow of my parting with so many, I send the order to Messrs. Hansard.

If a Member wishes for a number of copies of any particular Paper, or for a set of Papers, he will apply to The Speaker for an order?—Yes, he would.

London Gazette, 1817, vol. 1, p. 847.

House of Commons, April 5, 1817.—Notice is hereby given, that the Official Abstract of the daily proceedings of the House of Commons, and of the business appointed for next day, will be published at the rate of four pence per sheet, at No. 5, King-street, Westminster, for the remainder of the present Session.

The daily Votes will be delivered every morning, in town, for a guinea and a half, or sent, postage free, into the country for twenty-five shillings.

The Index to the Votes, at the end of the Session, or any occasional Appendix during the Session, will be furnished at four pence per sheet, if required.

Apply personally, or by letter (post paid), to James Mitchell, No. 5, King-street, Westminster.

Evidence.

Mr. Francis Wright, p. 35. Rep. 1828 (520.)

You are a Messenger of the House of Commons?—I am.

The Messengers of the House of Commons have always had a certain proportion of Papers delivered to them as a perquisite?—Yes.

Those they consider themselves entitled to dispose of as they think fit?—Yes. When I first came here, five-and-twenty years ago, I came as Extra Messenger, one of the first that was established. The four Messengers then on the establishment had those Papers and things of that kind; I then applied to the present Lord Colchester to know whether, as an Extra Messenger, I was not entitled to them; he sent for Mr. Dorington and for Mr. Babb, then at the Vote Office, and said that myself and the other Extra Messengers were to have the same as the other four had them; they have always been continued; how it was before that, I do not know.

If you have extra copies of the Acts of Parliament deposited in your hands, that the Members for whom they are intended do not want, you dispose of them in the same manner as those other Papers?—Yes; our salary is only 12*l.* 13*s.* 6*d.* a year. Myself and two of the other Messengers paid 500*l.* a piece for our situations. For the future all places, both Door-keepers and Messengers, will be given away; but there are myself and two others that are on the old establishment as having purchased.

Mr. J. H. Hansard, p. 76.

You do not make any additional charge for any number of additional copies you print of the Votes, but you charge as you have stated for 1,250 copies?—About 250 of those 1,250 copies are sold, and accounted for to the Public; there are 930, or thereabouts, delivered for the use of the Members, Public Offices, &c. and 250 are sold to solicitors and others; and those sold are accounted for in our bill.

Through whom are they sold?—They are all sold through the agency of Mr. Mitchell, who is the only authorized person; we do not sell any ourselves.

—6.—

Second Report on Public Documents; 13 *August* 1833. (717.)

The Right Hon. The Speaker. p. 46.

432. The two main objects of the present Committee are, first, to consider in what manner information can be afforded to the two Houses of Parliament, and to those among the Public who interest themselves in such matters, in a more regular and complete form than has hitherto been done; and in the second place, the printing and diffusing that information,

information, if possible, more economically; the Committee would be glad to hear from The Speaker any opinion or suggestion which he might have to make on either of those two heads?—With respect to the first, I do not think that I feel myself competent to offer any opinion to the Committee, as my opinion crudely arrived at would be of very little value. With respect to the latter, of the expense, it seems to me extremely difficult to know how, upon a general system, materially to diminish that. The expense principally arises from the printing ordered by The House. The system hitherto that has been pursued with respect to all Bills, and with respect to all Papers presented to The House, where they have been ordered to be printed, is this, 1,000 copies have been struck off, and if a larger number seems to be requisite, that has been by special direction of The Speaker, and The Speaker has always been governed in his directions upon that subject by looking to the character of the document to be so printed; first, whether it shall appear to excite a very large public interest, and secondly, whether it is likely in its interest to be merely ephemeral, or to continue a lengthened time. With respect to the first, it is obvious that it is material that as large a number should be printed off as should answer the purpose for The House, and for the information of those interested in it. With respect to the next point, The Speaker has always considered that the additional amount of printing involved only the expense of the paper, and might save the re-setting the press upon a subsequent occasion. It must be obvious to every one who considers it, that a great number of Papers and Reports and Accounts presented to The House, are not dealt with in the Session in which they are printed, but obviously hanging over for consideration in a future Session; the demand for those Papers therefore must be calculated as a demand for two Sessions. With these two objects in view, I have variously given directions to print from 1,500 to 3,000 copies; I can point out no particular reason that has guided me as a general rule, but I have always been governed by the peculiar subject on which the enlarged print has taken place.

Appendix, No. 4.

Evidence.

The Right Hon. The Speaker. p. 48. Rep. 1833 (717.)

433. Would there be any advantage, in your opinion, in order to meet cases where any general and extensive interest is excited, in having copies sold to the Public, and printed for that purpose?—I have no reason to think that inconvenience would be derived from that, and I know of no disadvantage from it, at the present moment; there is one Parliamentary Paper, pretty well known to every body, which is sold to the Public, and that is the Votes; I know not why other Parliamentary Papers should not be so disposed of to the Public, unless in cases where they involve the Privilege of The House, which of course must be rather exceptions; but on the other hand, it being well known that to the great majority of cases, with respect to Reports, for instance, unless from Secret Committees, persons may, by paying for them, get copies from the Journal Office, they being office copies, and that the distribution therefore is not confined to the Members of the House, I see no reason why the Public should not be accommodated with a print for sale, as they have a right now to be furnished with a manuscript copy.

434. What kind of Papers are they to which you now refer, of which office copies may be given on application?—On all Public Committees the parties may have office copies of either the entire or a part, on paying for them.

435. The authority to print the Evidence before Committees rests, the Committee believe, with The House, and not the Chairman of the Committee?—The Order is usually signed by The Speaker; the Chairman comes to The Speaker with a paper, desiring that the Evidence may be printed from day to day, for the use of the Members only; and I have given the strongest injunctions to the Printers, Messrs. Hansard, that they should not suffer any copies to get out, except those to be delivered to the Members; and I believe that the number of copies printed does not exceed the number of Members of the Committee by more than two or three, one of which very frequently The Speaker has, but not always. p. 47.

---

349. How many copies do you print in those instances?—For The House of Commons we generally print from 1,500 to 2,000 copies, and an extra 500 copies for the use of The Lords.

Messrs. Hansard. p. 40.

350. Therefore, in instances of Reports which you have printed for the use of The House of Lords, you have printed 2,500 copies?—Certainly.

351. You have nothing to do with the distribution of those copies which are delivered by you?—We deliver a certain stipulated number to the Vote Office, which is charged with the distribution of them to the Members, and the remainder of them are kept in store by us for the use of The House, under the direction of The Speaker, as they are from time to time required.

352. When you print for the use of The House of Lords, do you deliver the whole 500 to any officer of the House of Lords?—We deliver them to the Printer of The House of Lords.

353. How many do you send to the Vote Office on ordinary occasions?—On ordinary occasions we send 913 copies, that is, when 1,000 copies only were ordered; in extraordinary cases, such as those instances where larger numbers are printed, we send from about 1,000 to 1,200; if a greater number are required for distribution to Members, then additional numbers are supplied by the special Order of The Speaker.

354. Do you generally receive any direction as to the number that you are to print?—The directions are general; the standard number is 1,000 for all matters of an ordinary description; when they exceed that number, we have special directions from The Speaker.

Appendix, No. 1.

Evidence.

Messrs. *Hansard.* p. 40.

Rep. 1833 (717.)

365. But generally speaking, as regards a Bill, or as regards the Report of a Committee, if you receive no special order, do you print 1,000 copies?—If we receive no special orders, we print 1,000 copies, unless the Report or Evidence we are printing is a continuation of a preceding Report, or continuation of the evidence of a preceding Session, then we print the same number as we printed the preceding Session, in order that the sets may be made perfect. The practice is this; when a Report is going to press, of any description different from the ordinary course of business, the Report is laid before The Speaker, requesting his direction of the number of copies that are to be printed; that is done through the Clerk of the Journals, and from him we receive the directions of the number that are to be printed.

366. Does it happen frequently that you receive an order of that sort; does it happen periodically?—It happens whenever a Report is presented to The House from a Committee; for instance, when the Report of this Committee shall be presented to The House, the Report is shown to The Speaker, and he then writes an order for 1,500 copies; but, generally, that takes place at the close of the Session, because it has been the practice of Committees of The House to receive evidence during nearly the whole of the Session, and then near the termination of the Session, when these Reports are finally going to the press, we make a general list of such Reports, and upon that list we receive the final direction, from The Speaker, of the number to be printed.

367. Is it at the discretion of The Speaker to order as many to be printed as he thinks proper?—I presume so.

380. None of those 1,500 copies are distributed but under the direction of The Speaker?—Certainly not, after the first thousand are delivered at the Vote Office.

p. 41.

381. Will the expense of printing 2,500 copies of these East India Reports be very considerable?—Yes, certainly, they are very voluminous.

382. Was it by an Order of The Speaker this 2,500 were printed?—Certainly.

p. 42.

398. Can you state to the Committee how many copies of the Reports of the Charity Commissioners were printed by Order of The Speaker?—Two thousand five hundred copies of each, I think.

Report 1833 (717.)

Appendix, No. 2. p. 61.

An Account of the Expenses of printing the Votes and Appendix to the Votes of The House of Commons, for the Year ending 1830; and the Money received from Sale to the Public.

Session 1830.

VOTES.	£.	s.	d.	APPENDIX.	£.	s.	d.
Printing - - - -	1,706	–	–	Printing - - - -	957	18	–
Paper - - - - -	691	6	–	Paper - - - -	513	–	–
	2,397	6	–		£. 1,470	18	–
Received of Mr. Mitchell, (Votes sold to the Public)	659	3	–				
	£. 1,738	3	–				

J. B. Nichols & Son.

Report 1833 (717.) p. 6.

Total Expense of Printing for the last Three Years, £. 195,772.

It appears to Your Committee that a considerable Saving might be made in this large item of Expenditure:—

By permitting the Papers, Reports, &c. to be sold to the Public, in the same manner that is now adopted with respect to the Votes. The Committee refer to the Accounts of Messrs. Nichols, to show that 400 *l.* or 500 *l.* are annually received from Mr. Mitchell on this head.

p. 7.

Your Committee would recommend that the *Journals* for any past years should, if in the store and wanted by the Members or any other person, be sold in the same manner as the Votes or Parliamentary Papers.

— 7. —

Report on House of Commons' Offices and Fees; 10 August 1833. (648.)

Evidence.

Mr. W. Bellamy. p. 111.

1683. You receive a set of Votes and Parliamentary Papers?—Yes.
1684. Under what authority?—I do not know; it has been usual.
1685. Do you sell them?—I have sold them, and I have not sold them.

Mr. *Chas. Poulain.* p. 112.

1710. There is also an item of 1,547 *l.* 17 *s.* for sets and partial sets of Papers given to the office by Members, sets unclaimed by Members, official persons, &c.; what are the particulars of this item?—Those are the sets of Papers sold to the public.

1711. Are

Appendix, No. 4.

Evidence.

Mr. Chas. Public. Rep. 1833 (648.)

1711. Are they sold by the sheet?—They are generally sold in complete sets, at eight guineas and a half for the Session.

1712. The Papers and Votes?—No, the Papers only; the Votes are three guineas, and the Appendix 4 *d.* per sheet; the amount, therefore, for the Appendix, differs every Session.

1713. Do you charge two guineas and a half for delivery in that case?—No.

1714. You make a charge of two guineas and a half to a Member for sending his Papers into the country, but if you sell those Papers to strangers you do not charge that?—No, the delivery is included in the eight guineas and a half.

1715. Was there not an Order of The House, giving permission to you to sell the Votes?—Yes; Mr. Mitchell was authorised by The House, as the Publisher of the Votes and Appendix.

1716. In that Order, were you not to account to the Public for the sale of them?—Yes.

1717. Do you do so?—Yes; Mr. Mitchell pays Mr. Nichols 700 *l.* or 800 *l.* a Session in abatement of Mr. Nichols' account for printing.

1718. The House have not authorised the sale of Papers?—Not in the same way.

1719. Do you also sell some Votes?—Yes; Mr. Mitchell is the publisher.

* * * * * * * *

1756. It is stated in the Return, that a large sum of money is received for sets and partial sets of Papers, given to the Office by Members; have you or Mr. Mitchell a right to keep any other Papers on your own account, than merely those which fall into your hands from not being called for?—There are 50 sets which have been put aside under established usage, as the perquisite of the Office; the remainder of the sets sold are made up from those which some Members give; there are also Members who only take their Votes, and some Irish Members take only Irish Papers; and other Members do not require Irish Papers, but only English; consequently the Irish of one Member, and the English of another, make sets. p. 114.

1757. You receive eight guineas and a half for a set of Papers?—Yes, that is the sum Mr. Mitchell receives.

1758. What is the amount of the whole of Mr. Mitchell's perquisites in the shape of 50 sets of Papers, Votes, Appendix, &c.?—I should think between 700 *l.* and 800 *l.* a year.

1759. That is independent of other Papers which come into his hands in consequence of Members not claiming them?—Yes; those 50 sets he found as a perquisite of the Office when he came to it. Mr. Babb, his predecessor, likewise did the same. What the original authority for that was we cannot tell.

1760. It has been the custom occasionally to deliver the Papers of The House of Commons to some official persons, which have been discontinued; do they become Mr. Mitchell's?—Yes; all in the Speaker's list which are not taken up become the perquisite of the Office.

1761. What number of copies do they amount to?—They would probably amount to, I should think, 40 or 50.

1762. That comes to about 600 *l.* or 700 *l.* more?—Yes.

1763. The Papers he receives as the perquisites of his office being 50 copies, and from 40 to 50 copies, the delivery of which has been discontinued, amount to from 1,300 *l.* to 1,400 *l.* a year?—Yes.

1764. Has he sufficient sale for the Papers he has to sell?—Yes, he has applications for more.

1765. What is the probable amount of Papers left by Members, what number of sets?—That I can scarcely speak to at present; I should say, perhaps, not more than 12 or 14 complete sets, or 20 at the outside.

1766. That is independent of the 50 and the 40?—Yes.

1767. Altogether they are equal to about 100 sets?—Yes.

1768. Could a considerable quantity more be sold if The House permitted it?—Yes, I should think so.

1769. To a very large amount?—That I cannot say. Many applications are made for complete sets, and others only for particular Papers.

1770. Would a considerable benefit be made from the sale of Papers, if permitted by The House?—I think that is very doubtful. If they were regularly sold to the public, there must be always a sufficient number printed to supply the public.

1771. What right do you conceive Mr. Mitchell has to sell those Papers formerly delivered to persons whose offices have been abolished?—He found it the practice when he came to the office. The Speaker was acquainted with it.

1772. Have not some others been discontinued since he came to office?—Yes.

1773. On what ground did he sell those?—Because it had been done so in other instances. His predecessor, Mr. Babb, of course told him the custom of the office.

1774. What authority has Mr. Mitchell for selling those Papers?—The same as I have before stated, long-established usage, and with the knowledge of The Speaker.

1775. Supposing an office were abolished to-morrow, would Mr. Mitchell consider himself entitled to sell those Papers for his own private use?—Yes; that has been the custom for many years.

1776. The sum received for a complete set of Papers being eight guineas and a half, does that include everything printed by the Order of The House?—Yes; Papers, Bills, Reports and Returns.

1777. Considering the number of Papers printed by Order of The House, is not the eight guineas and a half less than the prime cost of the Papers?—I should think so. p. 115.

Appendix, No. 4.

Evidence.

Mr. Chas. Pushin, p. 115.

1778. Supposing The House were to permit them to be sold at a fair profit on the printing of them, do you conceive that many sets could be sold?—I should think that there might.

Rep. 1833 (648.)

Appendix, No. 1. p. 139.

A Return of the Amount of the Salaries, Fees and other Emoluments of Mr. James Mitchell, Deliverer of the Votes and Printed Papers.

	£.	s.	d.
Salary, paid by the Treasury - - - - - - - - -	14	12	6
Fees for the delivery of Votes, Papers, &c.; presents from Members, &c.	1,956	17	–
Sets and partial sets of Papers given to the office by Members; sets unclaimed by officers, persons, &c. - - - - - - -	1,547	17	–
	3,519	6	6
Deduct, salary of official deputy, three clerks, ten office porters, retired allowance to late assistant, &c. - - - - - - -	1,694	12	6
£.	1,824	14	–

Evidence.

Messrs. Hansard. p. 203.

3045. If the House of Commons should think that no Papers should be sold from the Vote Office, do you think there would be a difficulty in making an arrangement on your part, by which Papers might be sold to the public at a fair price?—There would be no difficulty.

3046. You would have no difficulty in undertaking that the public should be supplied at a fair rate?—None whatever.

3047. Do you conceive that the rate to be fixed by you should be submitted to The Speaker, or to some person who should sign it, and see that the rate is fair?—Certainly.

The Vote Office.

Report, p. 11.

The manner in which the officers in this department are remunerated appears very objectionable, and extremely expensive to the public, as a considerable proportion of the emoluments of the principal officer arise from the Sale of Papers printed at the public expense, of which he receives a large quantity, either as a perquisite of office, as belonging to Members, or for public offices which have been abolished, or which do not require the Papers to which they are entitled, and which are then, by the custom of the office, deemed to be a perquisite.

This system has prevailed for many years, and no blame is therefore attributable to the principal of this office. Your Committee, however, consider that no public officer should be allowed to dispose, for his own benefit, of any Papers printed at the public expense, and therefore recommend that the custom should be abolished, and that no Papers printed by the order of The House should be allowed or delivered to any of the clerks or officers, except such as may be necessary for their official use.

— 8. —

Second Report on Printed Papers; 18 July 1835. (392.)

Report, p. xiii.

It appears very desirable that the public should be supplied with the Parliamentary Sessional Papers in the same way as they are supplied with the Votes; and the annually increasing demand for these Votes leads Your Committee to believe, that if the Sessional Papers were sold at fixed and moderate prices, and facilities given for their sale, that many of them would be purchased for the use of public libraries, reading-rooms and public associations, and also by many public bodies and private individuals.

The information which The House intended to convey by the printing of their Returns and Papers, has hitherto been too much confined to its Members; but the advantage to the community by the diffusion of that information which can, in the generality of cases, be obtained only through the House of Commons, must be evident to every Member who has directed his attention to the subject; and the estimation in which such information is held

held by public and private institutions, must be considered as a proof of its value, and a demand for its circulation. At present, 100 or more sets of Sessional Papers are sold at the Vote Office; but the demand of the public is supplied chiefly by Members giving their own copies, or by their procuring, by order of The Speaker, copies for their constituents and friends; a means of supply most unsatisfactory in many respects; and Your Committee concur in opinion with preceding Committees who have called the attention of The House to the subject, that means should be provided for selling them as the Votes are sold. Appendix, No. 5. — Rep. 1835 (392.) p. xxiii.

In December 1834, Messrs. Hansard, in obedience to the Orders of The Speaker, to take into consideration the best means of carrying into effect the suggestions of the Committee, submitted their views of the rate of charge and the means of sale, to which Your Committee must refer for details. They state that the charge of the Sessional Papers to the public, on the average of 1,500 copies, is 1d. per sheet; that they might be sold for 1½d. per sheet, and that an allowance of 17 per cent. might be made to booksellers for the retail. A table of the proposed prices is given, by which a Paper of 80 pages or 20 sheets would not exceed 1s. 6d., and one of 200 sheets or 800 pages, 25s., being equal in quantity to three volumes octavo at 12s. each; they observe that Papers having maps or plans may be sold at 2d. or 3d. per sheet, according to the cost. But as some of the small tabular Returns are more expensive in printing, and also more in request by the public, whilst the larger Reports would be of less account, it is suggested that a rate or price might be fixed higher for the small than for the larger, so as to return the average price of 1½d. per sheet, which is all that should be required by The House. Mr. Rickman expressed an opinion that the sale of the Papers should be by a shop, with an establishment of clerks, being opened by the Printers, and that they should only receive their actual expenses; but Your Committee are of opinion that the sale on commission and in different parts of the metropolis, would be the preferable mode both for The House, the public, and the parties who sell. There does not appear any reason why Messrs. Hansard, the Printers, should have the trouble of sale and custody without a fair remuneration; and they consider the amount of sale to be so uncertain, that it will be better to make the trial by agency and commission than by the formation of an establishment for that purpose. Your Committee examined several booksellers as to the sale of these Papers, and find that there will be no difficulty in obtaining respectable agents for the sale of the Papers, at a per centage of from 10 to 30 per cent., the Papers being taken on sale and return. Your Committee, considering the great and increasing accumulation of printed Parliamentary Papers in store, as already stated, and looking to the heavy expense incurred for printing, for warehouse rent, for establishment to take care of them, and taking into account the risk of fire, and of their being eventually fit only for waste paper, direct the particular attention of The House to these matters, with a view of checking, for the future, the charges now incurred; and, looking to the immense number of Sessional Papers now in store, exceeding two millions of copies, Your Committee recommend, *That the Reports and Parliamentary Papers printed for the use of The House, should be rendered accessible to the public by purchase, at the lowest possible price for which they can be furnished: that a sufficient number of copies should be printed for that purpose; and that they should be sold by agents in the metropolis, from whom the country demand may be supplied.* Report, p. xxiii. — Sale of Reports and Papers.

The orders for printing, preservation and delivery of the Votes, Parliamentary Papers, Reports and Journals, &c. have heretofore been under the special control of Mr. Speaker; and it has been under the consideration of Your Committee how far he should be assisted in and relieved from that duty. It appears to Your Committee that his power should still be exercised as regards the Votes and Proceedings of The House, the number of Bills and all such Papers as may be required for the current service of The House; but Your Committee are of opinion that a Select Committee, consisting of eight Members, of whom three should be officially connected with Government, be appointed at the commencement of each Session of Parliament, to assist The Speaker as to the printing, selection and delivery of Papers; that the Committee should meet once a week at the least; and, having before them every Return presented to The House, with the number and distribution of similar Papers printed in preceding years, and also such further information as Members calling for those Papers may afford; should decide on the number of copies to be printed for the use of The House, and also whatever number might be required to supply the official departments, and for sale to the public, as recommended in another part of the Report.

Appendix, No. 4.

Evidence.

Messrs. *Hansard*, p. 32.
Rep. 1833 (392.)

798. Have you turned your attention to the sale of Parliamentary Papers?—At the close of last year Sir Charles Manners Sutton directed us to put our thoughts together on the subject; in consequence of which, we made a statement to him, suggesting a plan of sale, and proposing a scale of prices; upon which Mr. Rickman was likewise required to make his observations. In these a lower scale is proposed, and other hints on the manner of conducting the sale, and defraying the attendant expenses. A further communication took place on our part, in which we offered our services in any way in which they might be thought useful. The correspondence on this subject I will leave with the Committee.

— 9. —

Third Report on Printed Papers (as to House of Commons' Offices), 7 *Sept.* 1835. (606).

VOTE OFFICE.

Rep. 1835 (606.) p. 9.

IT appears that the receipts of the Vote Office in 1832 were 3,518 *l.*, which may be taken as the average annual income, and was thus apportioned; viz.—To Mr. Mitchell, the head of the office, 1,824 *l.*; to the clerks, 1,000 *l.*, and to porters, messengers and other contingent expenses, 494 *l.*; and to Mr. Bastaff, a retired clerk, an annuity of 200 *l.*

Your Committee beg to call the attention of The House to the sources from which this income was derived:—1st, a salary of 14 *l.* from the Treasury; 2d, from fees from Members for the delivery of Sessional Votes and Papers, 1,957 *l.*; and 3d, by the sale of 100 sets of Parliamentary Sessional Papers, 1,548 *l.*; by which latter transaction the public sustained a loss of 1,200 *l.*, the Papers being sold for 12 *l.* per set less than their cost to the public for printing.

The Committee which sat in 1833, objected to this mode of remuneration, stating, "That no public officer should be allowed to dispose, for his own benefit, of any Papers printed at the public expense; and recommend, that the custom should be abolished, and that no Papers printed by order of The House should be allowed, or delivered to any of the clerks or officers, except such as may be necessary for their official use." And Your Committee are informed by Mr. Pashlo, now in charge of the Vote Office, that no change has as yet been made in that respect; they therefore concur with the former Committee *in recommending, that this objectionable practice be forthwith abolished.*

— 10. —

Resolution of the House of Commons on the 13th August 1835.

Journals, vol. 90, p. 544.

Resolved, THAT the Parliamentary Papers and Reports printed for the use of The House should be rendered accessible to the public by purchase, at the lowest price they can be furnished; and that a sufficient number of extra copies shall be printed for that purpose.

— 11. —

Martis, 9° *die Februarii*, 1836.

Journals, vol. 91, p. 16, and vol. 92, p. 17.

Ordered, THAT a Select Committee be appointed to assist Mr. Speaker in all matters which relate to the printing executed by order of The House, and for the purpose of selecting and arranging for printing, Returns and Papers presented in pursuance of motions by Members of the House, which may be referred to the said Committee.

— 12. —

Resolutions of the Committee on Printing, Friday, 18*th March* 1836.

1. THAT the Parliamentary Papers and Reports, and also the Votes, and Appendix to the Votes, should be sold to the public at the price of one halfpenny per sheet.

2. That all charts, plans or drawings which these Papers may contain, be charged at the rate of 3 *d.* for each half sheet, of 6 *d.* for each whole sheet of foolscap size, and 1 *s.* per sheet of larger size.

3. That

3. That Papers of former Sessions now remaining in store be sold at the same rate as those of the current Session.

4. That Messrs. Hansard, the Printers of the House, be appointed to conduct the sale.

5. That, in order to render the Parliamentary Papers accessible to the public through the means of other booksellers, it is expedient that a discount of 12½ per cent. should be allowed to the trade who shall become purchasers.

6. That this Committee recommend that Messrs. Hansard should charge in their accounts the actual expense incurred by them in carrying on the sale as proposed in these Resolutions.

April 22, 1836.

The Committee directed the Journals to be sold, at the rate of 10 s. per volume.

Appendix, No. 5.

Appendix, No 5.

List of Reports, 1680—1836, of a Criminatory Tendency.

LIST of REPORTS and PAPERS Printed by Order of the House of Commons, from 1680 to 1836, containing matter of a Criminatory Tendency.

1680. REPORT on the Impeachment of Sir William Scroggs and others.
— Report on the Impeachment of Thompson and others.

1696. Report on the Examination of the Conspirators in Newgate.

1696 to 1712. Several Reports on the Abuses in Prisons and pretended Privileged Places—Extortion of Gaolers—Bribery—Defiance of the Law.

1698. Report and Articles of Impeachment of Goudet.

1700. Report on Irish Forfeitures.

1702. Evidence on the Charge against the Bishop of Worcester for influencing an Election.
— Report of Commissioners of Accounts.

1710. Report on the Mine Adventure Company.
— Report on Abuses in the Victualling Department.
— Report on Imprest Accountants.

1711. Report of Commissioners of Public Accounts.

1715. Report of the Committee of Secrecy, on the Impeachment of Lord Bolingbroke.
— Report on Mr. Harley's Conduct.
— Report and Impeachment of Earl Derwentwater.
— Report on Poor and Scavengers' Rate in Westminster—Abuses in the Application of Rates—Mortality of Children with Parish-Nurses, from Mismanagement.

1716. Report from Commissioners on Forfeited Estates.

1719. Report of Inquiry into certain Subscription Projects.

1720. Report respecting the South Sea Company.

1722. Report on Layer's Conspiracy.

1723. Papers relating to the Conspirators.

1728. Report on the State of Gaols, and Abuses therein.

1732. Report on the Sale of the Derwentwater Estates.
— Report on the Management of the Charitable Corporation.

1733. Report on the Management of the York Buildings Company.
— Report on Frauds in the Customs.

1738. Report on the Management of the County Rates in Middlesex—Alleged Misapplication and Embezzlement by Magistrates.

1742. Report on the Conduct of the Earl of Orford; and Charges of Misapplication of the Public Money for Election Purposes.—Refusal of Mr. Paxton, Solicitor of the Treasury, to account.

1746. Report on the State of the Land Forces and Marines—Abuses in the Method of providing Clothing; in the Muster-rolls for drawing Pay; and Misapplication of Paymasters' Balances.

Appendix, No. 5.

List of Reports, 1680—1838, of a Criminatory Tendency.

1752. Report on Turnpike Road Trusts—Misapplication of Funds, and Defalcation of Officers entrusted with them.

1754. Report on the Management of the Lottery for disposing of the Sloanean Collection—Undue preference in the subscription of the Tickets.

1763. Reports on the Management of Private Madhouses—Illegal Confinement of Persons, and culpable Treatment of Patients.

1763-4. Reports on the Misapplication of Funds of Highway Trusts.

1772 to 1783. Reports on the Affairs of the East India Company—Abuses in the Administration of Civil and Criminal Justice—The Exercise of Political and Military Power—The Abuse of Civil Power—Oppression of Native Chiefs—Exaction of Presents—Conduct of Lord Clive, Sir Thomas Rumbold, Warren Hastings, Esq., and other Servants of the Company.

1783. Report on Frauds and Abuses in the Victualling Department at Portsmouth.

1783-4. Report on Smuggling and other Illicit Practices used in defrauding the Revenue.

1794. Report on Charges against Mr. Warren Hastings.

1799. Report on the State of Coldbath-fields Prison—Complaints of Colonel Despard.

— Report on Seditious Societies.

1805. Report on the Treasurership of the Navy, and Charges against Lord Melville.

1806-7. Report respecting the Return of Mr. Cawthorne.

1809. Report on the Disposal of the Patronage of the East India Company, by Mr. Thellusson.

— Report on the Management of Coldbath-fields Prison—Alleged Ill-treatment of the Prisoners.

— Report of Evidence on Charges against the Duke of York, by Mrs. Mary Ann Clarke.

1810. Papers respecting the Treatment of Slaves, by Mr. Huggins, at St. Nevis.

1811. Papers respecting Reflections on the Conduct of Mr. Garnett and others, in relation to the Trial of Mr. Huggins, at St. Nevis.

— Report on the State of Lancaster Prison—Complaints of Messrs. Finnerty and Drakard.

1813. Papers respecting the Conduct of the Governor of Grenada, in punishing a coloured Inhabitant.

1814-15. Papers respecting Complaints of the Government of Gloucester Gaol, and the Treatment of Prisoners confined therein.

1814 to 1822. Several Reports on the State of Prisons and the Conduct of Gaolers.

1814-15. Report respecting the Return and Arrest of Lord Cochrane.

1814 to 1828. Several Reports on the State and Management of Lunatic Asylums—Alleged Abuses.

1816 to 1819. Return of Persons accused of Frauds on the Excise Laws.

1816. Charges brought against Lord Ellenborough by Lord Cochrane, concerning the Trial of De Berenger and others.

1816 to 1833. Reports and Papers respecting the Employment of Children in Cotton Factories.

1817-18. Reports on Seditious Practices.

1819 to 1834. Reports of Commissioners of Charities and Education.

1820. Report on Abuses of the Corporation of Limerick.

1821. Charges against J. Pollock, Esq., founded on the Second Report of the Commissioners of Inquiry into the Courts of Justice in Ireland.

1822. Report on Printing and Stationery.

— Reports on the State of the Colony of New South Wales—Conduct of the Governor and Persons employed by him.

— Report on the Local Taxation of the City of Limerick—Misapplication of the Revenues and Defalcation of the Treasurer.

1822. Report

Appendix, No. 5.

List of Reports, 1820—1836, of a Criminatory Tendency.

1821. Report on the Management of Ilchester Gaol—Complaint of Mr. Hunt.

— Return of Defaulters in Public Accounts.

— Abstract of Report of Colonial Auditors as to the Accounts of Mr. Theodore Hook.

1823. Papers respecting the Treatment of Slaves at Honduras; alleged Cruelties practised, with Details of Cases, and specific Accusations.

1824. Several Papers on the same subject.

1825. Report on the Abuses in the Management of Bradford Gaol.

1825–26. Minutes of Evidence and Papers on the Petition of M. M. Conlor, respecting Mr. Kenrick's Conduct as a Magistrate.

1826. Report on the Management of the Paving Board, Dublin—Misapplication of Money by the Collectors.

1826–27. Papers respecting the Ill-treatment of a Female Slave by Mr. Carden, at Jamaica.

1826. Thirteenth and Fourteenth Reports of the Commissioners of Revenue Inquiry, as to the Conduct of Mr. Sedgwick and Mr. Barber Beaumont.

1827. Report on the Management of the Arigna Mining Company.

1829. Papers respecting the Ill-treatment of a Female Slave, by Henry and Ellen Moss, of Crooked Island, Bahamas.

— Report on the Conduct of Mr. Nash in regard to the granting Crown Leases, and making Contracts for executing Works at Buckingham Palace.

1829. Report relating to the Charges against Sir Jonah Barrington, for Misconduct in the discharge of his Judicial Functions.

1830–31. Papers respecting the Ill-treatment of a Female Slave in Jamaica by the Rev. Mr. Bridges.

— Papers respecting the reported Ill-treatment of a Slave, named Henry Williams, in Jamaica.

1831–32. Papers relating to the Punishment of two Female Slaves belonging to Mr. Jackson, Custos of Port-Royal.

1831. Report on the Mode of supplying Furniture for Windsor Castle; Charges made by Messrs. Morel and Seddon in their Accounts.

1832. Report on the Abolition of Slavery.

1833. Reports respecting the Stationery-office, on the Conduct of Sir John Key.

— Report on Liverpool Election.

— Report on Hertford Election.

— Report on Stafford Election.

1833–34. Reports on the State and Conduct of the Police of the Metropolis.

— Factory Commissioners' Reports.

1834. Reports on the Administration of the Poor Laws.

1834–35. Reports on the State and Management of Municipal Corporations (England and Ireland).

1835. Report on Bribery and Intimidation at Elections.

— Reports on Orange Lodges.

— Report on the Conduct of General Darling and Petition of Captain Robison.

— Report on Yarmouth Election.

— Report on York Election.

— Report on Chatham Election.

1836. Report on the Management of the British Museum.

— Report on the Management of the Record Commission.

— Report on Carlow Election.

— Report on Poole Borough Election.

— Reports of Inspectors of Prisons. (*That on the State of Newgate is the Report which gave rise to the Action* Stockdale v. Hansard, *and the opinion of* Lord Denman *as to the liability of persons dispersing Parliamentary Papers to Actions for Libels.*)

N.B. *The Reports on Elections, above mentioned, are distinct from Reports on Controverted Election Petitions, which are not inserted in this List.*

APPENDIX.

LIST OF APPENDIX.

www.ingramcontent.com/pod-product-compliance
Lightning Source LLC
Chambersburg PA
CBHW031409160426
43196CB00007B/951
* 9 7 8 3 7 4 1 1 9 8 6 6 3 *